I0434826

S. HRG. 113–491

BLM PERMIT PROCESSING

HEARING

BEFORE THE

COMMITTEE ON ENERGY AND NATURAL RESOURCES UNITED STATES SENATE

ONE HUNDRED THIRTEENTH CONGRESS

SECOND SESSION

ON

BREAKING THE LOGJAM AT BLM: EXAMINING WAYS TO MORE EFFI-
CIENTLY PROCESS PERMITS FOR ENERGY PRODUCTION ON FEDERAL
LANDS THE PURPOSE OF THIS HEARING IS TO UNDERSTAND THE
OBSTACLES IN PERMITTING MORE ENERGY PROJECTS ON FEDERAL
LANDS AND TO CONSIDER S. 279, THE PUBLIC LAND RENEWABLE EN-
ERGY DEVELOPMENT ACT OF 2013, AND S. 2440, THE BLM PERMIT
PROCESSING IMPROVEMENT ACT OF 2014, AND RELATED ISSUES

JULY 29, 2014

Printed for the use of the
Committee on Energy and Natural Resources

U.S. GOVERNMENT PRINTING OFFICE

91–553 PDF   WASHINGTON : 2014

For sale by the Superintendent of Documents, U.S. Government Printing Office
Internet: bookstore.gpo.gov Phone: toll free (866) 512–1800; DC area (202) 512–1800
Fax: (202) 512–2104 Mail: Stop IDCC, Washington, DC 20402–0001

(II)

CONTENTS

STATEMENTS

APPENDIXES

APPENDIX I

APPENDIX II

BLM PERMIT PROCESSING

TUESDAY, JULY 29, 2014

U.S. SENATE,
COMMITTEE ON ENERGY AND NATURAL RESOURCES,
Washington, DC.

The committee met, pursuant to notice, at 2:34 p.m. in room SD–366, Dirksen Senate Office Building, Hon. Mary L. Landrieu, chair, presiding.

OPENING STATEMENT OF HON. MARY L. LANDRIEU, U.S. SENATOR FROM LOUISIANA

The CHAIR. Good afternoon.

I'd like to call our meeting of the Energy and Natural Resources Committee so that we can begin.

We have a very short period in which to give some opening remarks. There have been 4 votes called at 2:45. I understand one is a record vote, the other by voice vote.

So I'm going to open with a short statement, turn to you, Senator Tester, Senator Udall, when Senator Murkowski comes and if we can include Senator Barrasso, who's a lead sponsor of one of these bills, we will.

Let me just quickly say, good afternoon. Welcome to our committee. This hearing is focused on the job killing backlog of pending permits for energy production on Federal land.

A special welcome to Senator Tester and Senator Udall, who have been leaders in trying to break up this backlog, expedite permitting with a balance that is required and have in their bills some suggestions in which to accomplish that.

The bounty and beauty of the American West has stirred the hopes and dreams of generations of Americans. The vast economic potential of the West was only a dream in 1804 when President Thomas Jefferson sent Lewis and Clark on their now famous and well documented journey.

A little over 30 years later in 1837, Washington Irving published the epic following the adventures of the famous explorer, Captain Bonneville, in what would later become known as the Wyoming Territory. He searched for the fabled Tar Springs. After a great ordeal the men in his party discovered a slow stream of oil at the foot of a sand bluff just east of the Wind River Mountains.

Fifty years later a Pennsylvania born Irishman named Mike Murphy drilled the first well in the Wyoming Territory on the very same spot.

These examples of exploration and discovery began a transformation of American society that still rings true today. Today we have over 2.45 million acres of Western lands managed by the Bureau of Lands Management. It's so important that these lands are properly managed for the creation of wealth and prosperity for our Nation, the preservation of our environment and our way of life.

One of the ways that land is disturbing, however, is that it's taking over 200 days to review and approve new applications for permits to drill, called APDs. Under the current law the permit process is supposed to take only 30 days. We will explore the gap today.

At today's hearing we'll also hear about other obstacles that are creating these delays and how this committee, working together, can eliminate or reduce them.

We'll also explore some ideas how to best harness Federal lands for renewable energy production like wind, solar and geothermal.

I'm going to submit the rest of my statement to the record.

Senator Tester, you're welcome. Love you to begin. As soon as our colleague, Senator Udall, gets here we will turn to him for opening remarks.

Thank you so much for your leadership, your understanding of these issues, being from the State of Montana, and thank you for spending your time with us this afternoon.

[The prepared statement of Senator Tom Udall follows:]

PREPARED STATEMENT OF HON. TOM UDALL, U.S. SENATOR FROM NEW MEXICO

Chairwoman Landrieu, Ranking Member Murkowski, thank you for holding today's hearing S. 2440, the BLM Permit Processing Improvement Act of 2014. This bill is critical to continued energy development in the West. S. 2440 is bipartisan right down the middle—seven Democrats, seven Republicans, including Senators Barrasso, Henrich, Udall, Lee, Heller, and Hoeven on this committee. It is supported by the Western Governors' Association, by the Independent Petroleum Association of America, the American Petroleum Institute, and the American Oil and Gas Association. Kathleen Sgamma from the Western Energy Alliance is here to testify about her organization's support for the bill, as is Scott Kidwell of Concho Resources, the largest oil producer in New Mexico. We've heard from countless other oil and gas companies, large and small, who have expressed their support for this bill and the need to enact the law this year. BLM Director Neil Kornze is here to convey the Bureau's support for this bill.

S. 2440 extends indefinitely a successful program from the Energy Policy Act of 2005. Section 365 of the EPACT authorized through 2015 a pilot program to provide additional resources to seven of the busiest field offices in the West, including two in my state-Carlsbad and Farmington. Last March, I visited with the BLM and energy producers in Carlsbad. One of the producers I met with told me that Carlsbad is the most effective office he's dealt with. Carlsbad has used the additional resources to hire more staff, work more closely with sister agencies, more through environmental review, and cut processing time to less than half of the national average. It is one of the busiest, and most effective, BLM offices in the nation. S. 2440 supports the work of the Carlsbad and Farmington offices, and by allowing the Secretary to designate new permit improvement offices to receive these funds, the bill ensures that the BLM can be responsive to new plays and changes in industry activity.

S. 2440 also provides certainty for both the BLM and industry. For the BLM, it provides certainty that the funds needed to meet its oil and gas permitting obligations will be there. The harsh cuts of sequestration, coupled with the looming expiration of the pilot office program, have had a chilling effect on oil and gas processing throughout the west, including New Mexico. Positions are left unfilled, and investments in technological improvements are being delayed. This has carried over into other aspects of the BLM's oil and gas mission, such as lease sales and inspection/enforcement activity. This bill gives the BLM the security to hire the staff and make the investments needed to process oil and gas permits efficiently and with thorough environmental review. The last thing any of us want is a return to the "check the box" approach to oil and gas permitting.

For industry, the bill provides certainty as to cost and timing of oil and gas permits. It sets an APD fee that is almost 50% higher than the current fee but locks it in for 10 years. This, coupled with the continuation of the EPACT program, gives industry the assurance that the BLM will have the staffing resources it needs to efficiently process permits.

S. 2440 provides additional resources to the BLM without further burdening the American taxpayer. In fact, the bill is paid for entirely by industry. But the benefits for the taxpayer are incredible. In 2013, oil and gas production on Federal onshore mineral estate generated $3 billion in royalties. New Mexico's share was $479 million. This bill is good for the BLM, good for industry, and good for the American taxpayer.

I am pleased that this committee is also considering S. 279, Public Land Renewable Energy Development Act, introduced by Senators Tester and Heller. I am proud to cosponsor this bill, which streamlines the permitting process for renewable energy projects on public lands. Since 2009, the BLM has made great strides in permitting renewable energy on the public lands, but this new program has a lot of red tape. This bill cuts some of that red tape so that renewable energy projects will go through a similar permitting process as traditional energy resources. Critically, the bill also returns portions of royalty payments to local communities and supports investments in wildlife habitat.

Together, these two bills will help streamline energy production on our public lands, and furthers a "Do It All, Do It Right" Energy Policy to take on the twin threats of global climate change and American dependence on foreign oil. With policies that encourage the production of clean energy, we can create a clean energy economy that leads the world in producing the jobs of the future, while we continue to develop our oil and gas resources efficiently and in an environmentally sound way.

Chairwoman Landrieu, Ranking Member Murkowski—I thank you for considering these two important bills. I urge you to move them out of committee quickly for the consideration of the Senate as a whole.

STATEMENT OF HON. JON TESTER, U.S. SENATOR FROM MONTANA

Senator TESTER. Thank you for those kind comments, Chairman Landrieu and thank you for being in this position of Chairman of Energy and Natural Resources.

I would say the same for Ranking Member Murkowski if she was here, but let the record reflect that.

I know that both of you, the leaders of this committee, spend a lot of time working to make smart investments in our Nation's energy infrastructure and streamlining the permit process.

I'm happy to be here today to talk about a bill that does exactly that, my Public Land Renewable Energy Development bill has strong bipartisan support on this committee. I am proud to introduce it with many of the colleagues here today, Senator Heller and Senator Heinrich, along with the Udall cousins, Mark and Tom and Senator Risch.

The companion bill which is also bipartisan is to receive a hearing today in the House. This is a popular bipartisan piece of legislation that will move this country forward. That's because it does a lot of good things.

It does them in a balanced way that will grow our economy and create jobs.

It will protect our environment and fund wildlife habitat protection.

It will promote American energy security by tapping into some of the best renewable energy sites on public lands.

It gives the department, the departments of our Administration, the tools that they need to streamline the leasing process for renewable energy development on public land, similar to what we do for oil and gas development.

It sets aside 15 percent of the royalty revenues to expedite the permitting process and it reinvests half of the royalty revenues from these renewable energy projects into the hands of States and counties where the development occurs.

Most importantly, 35 percent of the royalty revenues will go toward projects that protect wildlife habitat from renewable energy development. Protecting our public lands and keeping them public is vital to this American economy. Outdoor recreation generates $650 billion annually in consumer spending in the United States, supports more than 6 million direct jobs. I believe the expansion of wind and solar development is compatible with public land protection.

America's wind energy potential is vast. When it is responsibly developed it can be a win for business, a win for communities and a win for wildlife.

As a Montanan and as a farmer I understand our Nation's love affair with our treasured landscapes. That's why I'm so very proud of this bill. It will responsibly develop our energy resources and ensure that the revenues benefit the States and counties of our treasured lands.

You talked about the job killing backlog. This bill will reduce that backlog.

Finally, Madame Chair, I understand that you're also going to be discussing a bill today by Senator Tom Udall, the BLM Permit Processing Improvement Act. I am a co-sponsor of that bill. It is a good piece of legislation.

The Energy Policy Act's pilot permitting office, one of them is located in Mile City. They do a great job out there and are absolutely critical to continuing the economic growth in the Bakken oil region of Eastern Montana. Fhat is why I strongly support that legislation as well.

Thank you very much, Madame Chair, Ranking Member Murkowski, for your time.

The CHAIR. Thank you very much, Senator Tester.

Senator Murkowski, for an opening statement.

STATEMENT OF HON. LISA MURKOWSKI, U.S. SENATOR FROM ALASKA

Senator MURKOWSKI. Thank you, Madame Chairman. Appreciate the hearing this afternoon. I'm glad that we can spend some time focused on the pace of BLM's permitting and some of the many steps that we can do to better expedite it.

I think that this is a particularly important topic because, clearly, we need to do all that we can to maximize energy and mineral production of all kinds on all of our lands and in an efficient and an effective manner.

We also know that based on reported statistics, based on what we see happening on State and private lands and even based on a recent Inspector General's report that BLM must clearly improve in this area.

In Alaska we face constant battles with the Administration as to whether or not our Federal lands will even be accessible. Just as one promising project in our national petroleum reserve finally reaches the permitting stage many of us are concerned that BLM's potential restrictions could render it uneconomic.

The two bills before us today take on our permitting challenges, I think, in a very effective manner.

S. 2440 proposes to make permanent the very successful BLM pilot program that has led to significant improvement in the speed with which applications for permits to drill, APDs, are processed. It provides the Interior Secretary with flexibility to designate new project offices to account for new oil and gas plays as well as shifting industry priorities.

It also directs the Secretary to consider publicly available industry reports in determining how to allocate resources to ensure that the BLM is being proactive instead of reactive.

S. 279, among other things, proposes to establish in the renewables arena, the same type of competitive leasing and royalty program that exists for offshore oil and gas production.

It also directs that a portion of the royalties be utilized for processing applications in local BLM offices.

Permitting efficiency is something that we should be tackling, as a committee, as a Senate and as a Congress. So I applaud the bipartisan leadership that we see in these bills. I look forward to the testimony of our witnesses today.

The CHAIR. Thank you very much.

Senator Heller and Senator Portman, Senator Heinrich, you all have joined us. I think Senator Heinrich you were the early bird.

Does anyone want to say any just brief remarks? Then I think we're going to break for the vote and then come back.

Senator, would you care to add anything?

STATEMENT OF HON. MARTIN HEINRICH, U.S. SENATOR FROM NEW MEXICO

Senator HEINRICH. Thank you, Madame Chair.

I just want to say both of these bills are really an example, a positive example, of how we can work together to produce energy more effectively on this committee. They're both bipartisan. They're both based on things that work. I'm really excited to see this hearing today.

I think these are bills that will positively affect the energy industry throughout the West. I'm looking forward to hearing from our witnesses.

The CHAIR. Senator Heller.

STATEMENT OF HON. DEAN HELLER, U.S. SENATOR FROM NEVADA

Senator HELLER. Thank you, Madame Chair. I want to thank you and the Ranking Member for this hearing.

I'd like to submit my comments, opening statement, for the record if there are no objections.

The CHAIR. Without objection.

Senator HELLER. But I'd also like to make one quick introduction, if I may.

We have with us the Nye County Commissioner, Lorinda Wichman, at the committee today. I'd like to welcome her here. She's a friend and an important leader in our State.

She works tirelessly, not only for her constituents in Nye County, but for the entire State on natural resource related issues. It's a pleasure to have her here. I want to thank her for making the cross country trip on such a short notice.

Nye County, her county, has some of the best sunshine for solar development in the entire country. We just need to get the Federal Government out of the way so it can be utilized.

So anyway, Madame Chairman, and to her, thank you very much for being here and for taking time.

Thank you.

The CHAIR. Thank you very much.

Senator Portman.

STATEMENT OF HON. ROB PORTMAN, U.S. SENATOR FROM OHIO

Senator PORTMAN. Madame Chair, thank you. I really appreciate your holding this hearing.

I listened to Senator Tester there for a moment as I came in. He's the Chair of our Subcommittee on Governmental Affairs that has held a number of hearings on this topic. I'm the Ranking Member.

One thing we talked about in that hearing on is the Federal Permitting Improvement Act of 2013 which is bipartisan and gets at this broader issue. There is a challenge out here, not just on public lands, but on private lands the United States continues to lag behind. We are now number 17 in the annual IMF study for the ease of doing business as it relates to the permits necessary to green light something, actually build something.

As we've already seen in some of the testimony here this morning, I'm sure on the public lands the average number of days and the amount of investment and time and effort it takes is even greater than on private lands. So I look forward to hearing the testimony today.

We will continue to push our broader Federal Permitting Improvement act. I think it makes a lot of sense. It's bipartisan and has a lot of just very sensible changes to the way the Federal permits go. But also I'm very interested in this legislation that relates directly to public lands, more specifically, BLM lands.

So thank you for your having this hearing. We look forward to the testimony.

The CHAIR. Thank you.

Senator Barrasso, unfortunately, I just got a note that Senator Udall is going to be unable to make the meeting. He is required for quorum in the Foreign Relations Committee.

So, Senator Barrasso, we'll hear from you. Then we'll break for the votes. Then we'll come back to hear our panel.

STATEMENT OF HON. JOHN BARRASSO, U.S. SENATOR FROM WYOMING

Senator BARRASSO. Thank you very much, Madame Chairman. Thank you for holding today's hearing.

Last month Senator Tom Udall and I introduced S. 2440, the BLM Permit Processing Improvement Act of 2014. This bipartisan piece of legislation would reauthorize and make permanent the Bureau of Land Management's pilot office program. Enacted in 2005 the program has helped provide BLM offices in Wyoming and other States the resources necessary to process oil and gas permits. The program is set to expire September 2015.

We need to reauthorize the program so the people of Wyoming and other States can create jobs, grow their economies.

For years Federal policies have put Federal lands at a competitive disadvantage with the State lands and private lands. This is especially true when it comes to oil and natural gas production.

Last month the Energy Information Administration, EIA, found that between 2012 and 2013 there was, "A 9 percent drop in Federal, onshore, natural gas production with most of the decreases in Wyoming."

EIA also found that since 2009 Federal onshore natural gas production has decreased by 16 percent, decreased 16 percent. In fact, EIA found that Federal onshore natural gas production makes up a smaller percentage of total U.S. gas production that it has in 10 years.

In 2003 Federal onshore natural gas production made up 35 percent of total U.S. gas production, but 10 years later in 2013, Federal onshore natural gas production made up only 16 percent of total U.S. gas production.

Federal onshore oil production also makes up a smaller percentage of total U.S. oil production than it has in 7 years.

While these numbers reflect new energy production on State and private lands, they also show that Federal lands are becoming less competitive with State and private lands. Energy production on Federal lands puts money in the Federal Treasury. It reduces our budget deficit. We could stop making—we should make it—we should stop making it harder to produce energy on Federal lands.

S. 2440 is one way to do that.

This bill would give local BLM offices the financial resources necessary to process oil and gas permits in a timely manner. It will also give BLM the ability to anticipate where permitting backlogs may develop in the future and take steps to prevent them from occurring.

So I want to thank Senator Udall and his leadership on this bill. He's been a great partner to work with.

I would also like to thank the 6 other Democrat co-sponsors and 6 other Republican co-sponsors, including Senator Heinrich, Senator Heller, Senator Hoeven, Senator Lee and Senator Mark Udall, who are all members of this committee.

I'd also like to thank the witnesses, especially welcome Mark Christensen, Chairman of the Campbell County Commissioners for coming here to testify all the way from Gillette, Wyoming.

Thank you very much, Madame Chairman. I look forward to the testimony.

The CHAIR. Thank you, Senator, for your leadership.

I think we're going to go ahead and take a break. They've called the vote. So the committee will stand in recess for about 15 minutes. We'll resume, hopefully, right at half past the hour.

[RECESS.]

The CHAIR. Ladies and Gentlemen, if you'll take your seats our meeting will come to order from a brief recess.

Director Kornze, you want to take a seat?

Director Kornze is a Bureau of Land Management for the Department of Interior. We've asked you to give 5 minutes opening remarks and take questions for this hearing.

So please proceed. Thank you.

STATEMENT OF NEIL KORNZE, DIRECTOR, BUREAU OF LAND MANAGEMENT, DEPARTMENT OF THE INTERIOR

Mr. KORNZE. Thank you, Chair, and other members of the committee.

The Department is proud to be playing a major role in the Nation's energy economy. In the realm of conventional energy we have good news to share in production, oil production from public lands is at a 10-year high.

We also have good news in the permitting realm. Permitting numbers have come down by about a third in the last two to 3 years. We also, through the hard work of BLM and other agencies, have nearly 7,000 APDs or drilling permits that have been approved and are sitting with industry today that are available for drilling with no further action by the Bureau of Land Management.

So if you compare that number to the fact that the average number of wells spud on public lands each year is about 3,000 there's about 2 years worth of headroom available to industry. We're very proud of providing that opportunity.

In the realm of leasing we also have a positive story to tell. Last year the Bureau of Land Management made 5.7 million acres of land available for leasing across the system. Yet only 19 percent of that land received a bid from industry. So in many cases we are outpacing industry demand when it comes to leasing.

When it comes to inspection and enforcement we have a less positive story to tell. General accounting—Government Accounting Office has been reviewing our program recently and has highlighted the fact that we are only accomplishing 60 percent of our high priority drilling inspections and roughly 82 percent of our high priority production inspections. So with a record number of wells on public lands, we have a great responsibility. We must do better.

As part of a solution we had put in front of Congress, through the budgets, the President's budget proposal, an inspection and enforcement fee system which would make sure that we can be responsive to industry need and that we can fulfill 100 percent of our inspection and enforcement need.

Briefly on renewable energy.

The Nation's renewable energy production has doubled during this Administration. The Bureau of Land Management is proud to be part of that effort. Through that we have helped authorize more than 50 utility scale, renewable energy projects, solar, wind and geothermal, that have the potential to produce over 14,000 megawatts of power.

Specifically on the two bills in front of us today, S. 2240, the BLM Permit Processing Improvement Act. We appreciate the bipartisan nature of this effort and Senators Udall and Barrasso introducing it very recently. The bill is important to the Bureau of Land

9

Management and the efforts seen in the Energy Policy Act of 2005 have made a difference in our ability to move drilling permits.

75 percent of the drilling activity in the permits that we see come into our offices come into the top 5 oil and gas offices within our system. So the ability to move resources to the high producing, the high need offices, makes a huge amount of difference to us.

The $9,500 APE fee and the ability to move that with inflation over the years is also greatly appreciated. That tracks much better with the cost of what it takes to do that work. We appreciate, overall, the greater flexibility in this legislation including the ability given the Secretary, the opportunity to look at which offices should be prioritized at any given time because the focus in the areas of high production change as we have seen over the last decade.

We look forward to working with the committee on some small and technical changes to that legislation.

S. 279, the Public Land Renewable Energy Development Act, we are also very favorable to this legislation. We see it as a shared vision with a lot of the work that the Department of the Interior and the Bureau of Land Management have completed through Administrative means in recent years.

BLM has worked extensively to develop what we call the Western Solar Plan or the Solar Programmatic EIS which identified 17 low conflict, high prospectivity areas around the West that are good for solar leasing. We're very pleased to see a competitive offering of the Dry Lake zone in Southern Nevada recently that produced over, nearly, $6 million in bids for the acres that were offered.

We look forward to working with the committee to mesh these BLM efforts and the programs that we've built including a competitive leasing rule that we're currently working on with the legislation's objectives. We see this as a step forward.

We appreciate the opportunity to share this testimony and look forward to answering any questions you might have.

[The prepared statement of Mr. Kornze follows:]

PREPARED STATEMENTS OF NEIL KORNZE, DIRECTOR, BUREAU OF LAND MANAGEMENT, DEPARTMENT OF THE INTERIOR

ON S. 2440

Thank you for the opportunity to testify on S. 2440, the Bureau of Land Management (BLM) Permit Processing Improvement Act of 2014 (Act), which would reauthorize and expand the BLM's oil and gas project offices. The BLM supports the goal of S. 2440 to improve coordination and processing of oil and gas use authorizations and to better conform the project office authority to permitting demands that shift over time—thus facilitating the safe, responsible, and efficient development of domestic oil and gas resources on Federal and Indian Land. The BLM would like to work with the sponsor and the Committee on technical and clarifying modifications to the bill.

Background

Since the beginning of the Obama Administration, the Department of the Interior (Department) has made it a priority to permit environmentally-sound development of conventional energy and mineral resources on the Nation's public lands. The Department has been at the forefront of the Administration's efforts, outlined in the Blueprint for a Secure Energy Future, to create jobs and to reduce the Nation's dependence on fossil fuels and oil imports.

The BLM administers over 245 million surface acres—more than any other Federal agency—which are located primarily in 12 western States, including Alaska, as well as approximately 700 million acres of onshore subsurface mineral estate throughout the Nation. The BLM, together with the Bureau of Indian Affairs (BIA), also provides permitting and oversight services on approximately 56 million acres of land held in trust by the Federal government on behalf of tribes and individual Indian owners.

The BLM administers a robust and responsible oil and gas program on Federal public lands. While oil and gas development is a market-driven activity, Federal onshore oil production is the highest it has been in a decade and has risen for the fifth year in a row. Indeed, Federal onshore oil production last year rose 7 percent from the previous year and has risen 30 percent since 2008. Production from Indian trust lands last year rose 47 percent from the previous year and has more than tripled since 2008. In FY 2013 the BLM generated over $3 billion in oil and gas revenue, with approximately half of this amount disbursed to the states from the oil and gas production on federal lands within their borders, and over $850 million for Indian tribes and individual Indian owners.

Onshore, nearly 36.1 million acres of Federal public land were under lease to oil and gas companies last year. Of those acres, only 12.6 million acres were actively producing oil and gas, though that is the highest acreage under production since 2008. Last year, the BLM held 30 separate oil and gas lease sales, offering 5.7 million acres for lease by industry, the most in a decade; industry submitted bids on fewer than one-in-five of these acres.

The BLM continues to offer leasing opportunities far in excess of industry demand. The BLM has scheduled 28 lease sales for 2014, and has already held 14 of those sales. The BLM continues to improve its system for responsibly permitting oil and gas operations. Since 2008 the BLM has approved more than 27,000 Applications for Permits to Drill (APDs). The average processing time for onshore APDs is the lowest it has been in eight years. Industry now has nearly 7,000 approved drilling permits that are ready for drilling but currently sitting unused. If you compare that figure against the fact that an average of about 3,000 wells are spud on public lands each year, it becomes apparent that industry has ample opportunities to develop leased resources.

As part of the BLM's ongoing efforts to ensure efficient processing of oil and gas permit applications, the BLM is preparing to implement a new automated tracking system that could reduce the review period for drilling permits and expedite the sale and processing of Federal oil and gas permits. The new system for drilling permits will track applications through the entire review process and quickly flag any missing or incomplete information industry applicants need to provide, greatly reducing the back-and-forth between the BLM and applicants to amend paper applications.

The BLM's top priority for oil and gas is to ensure that operations are conducted safely and responsibly. The BLM performs thousands of inspections each year on oil and gas leases to check for safe, environmentally responsible operations, and to ensure a fair return to the taxpayer. But with an oil and gas budget that has declined by roughly 20 percent since 2007 when accounting for inflation, the challenges are considerable.

The BLM intends to continue its emphasis on high priority production inspections, which are critical for ensuring proper accounting of the billions of dollars of oil and gas produced and associated royalties collected from the public lands. However, our current funding system limits our ability to effectively meet this responsibility and ensure protection of both environmental and economic resources. Between 2009 and 2012, the BLM completed only 60 percent of high priority drilling inspections and in FY 2013, we completed just 82 percent of high priority production inspections.

In response to these challenges, the President's FY 2015 budget proposal asks Congress for the authority to charge an inspection and enforcement fee that reflects the actual cost of performing this function in order to strengthen our inspection and oversight capability. This fee system will help the BLM become more responsive to industry needs while also improving production accountability and safety and environmental protection of oil and gas operations. A similar fee system was authorized by Congress for offshore oil and gas inspections and has proven to be a successful model for industry and the relevant agencies.

Energy Policy Act of 2005

Section 365 of the Energy Policy Act of 2005 (EPAct) established the Federal Permit Streamlining Pilot Project with the intent to improve the efficiency of processing oil and gas use authorizations and environmental stewardship on Federal lands. It designated the following seven pilot project offices: Miles City, Montana; Buffalo and Rawlins, Wyoming; Vernal, Utah; Grand Junction/Glenwood Springs, Colorado; and Farmington and Carlsbad, New Mexico. On December 26, 2013, President Obama signed PL 113-69, which expanded the boundaries of two of the project offices— Miles City, to include the expanding Bakken development, and Buffalo—in response to changing demand for development of Federal oil and gas resources.

Section 365 also established the Permit Processing Improvement Fund, an account that has varied from about $23 million to about $18 million annually, to support the pilot project for 10 years. Specifically, it directed 50 percent of the income derived from Federal onshore oil and gas lease rental payments outside of Alaska to the Fund. For FY 2006 through FY 2015, Section 365 made the Fund available to the Secretary of the Interior for expenditure without further appropriation to enhance coordination and processing of oil and gas use authorizations on Federal land under the jurisdiction of the designated pilot project offices.

In addition, Section 365 authorized the Secretary to transfer monies from the Permit Processing Improvement Fund as necessary for permit coordination and processing to other agencies involved in the process, including the U.S. Fish and Wildlife Service, the Bureau of Indian Affairs, the U.S. Forest Service, the Environmental Protection Agency, the Army Corps of Engineers, and the states of Wyoming, Montana, Colorado, Utah, and New Mexico. It also prohibited the BLM from establishing cost recovery fees for processing oil and gas drilling permits, although the Congress has implemented permit fees through annual appropriations language since 2007. The President's 2015 budget proposes to repeal this fee prohibition.

The agencies involved in the pilot project have made significant progress in a number of areas. Additional resources, such as personnel devoted to processing oil and gas use authorizations, have enabled the various bureaus and agencies to increase the pace of permitting and completing environmental reviews, particularly given the complex resource issues we face. The time taken for interagency consultations has been reduced due to improved communication and through programmatic streamlining efforts, which have been used in multiple projects and permits. The increased staffing in the pilot project offices has also allowed the BLM to help new industry permitting specialists understand the BLM's requirements for obtaining an oil and gas use authorization.

In FY 2013, the top ten BLM offices with the highest industry interest in oil and gas development on Federal and Indian Lands managed over 86 percent of the total APDs processed during the year. However, only four of those offices were among the originally identified pilot offices.

S. 2440

S. 2440 reauthorizes and expands the BLM's oil and gas project office program. The bill would amend the Energy Policy Act of 2005 to extend the use of oil and gas lease rental receipts from the BLM Permit Processing Improvement Fund through 2026 for the coordination and processing of oil and gas use authorizations in BLM's oil and gas project offices. Also, under the bill, the geographic scope of the oil and gas project office program would be expanded to include any BLM State, district, or field office as determined appropriate by the Secretary to improve use authorization coordination and processing. The bill would establish a $9,500 APD processing fee indexed for inflation through 2026, and would prohibit the Secretary from implementing a rulemaking that would enable an increase in fees to recover additional costs related to processing APDs. Finally, the bill would require an annual report on the allocation of funds and the accomplishments of each project office.

The BLM supports the reauthorization and expansion of the agency's oil and gas pilot office program, which has been extremely valuable in improving oil and gas permit coordination and processing. The BLM supports the expanded geographic scope provided by the bill which will allow the BLM to better allocate resources based on current permitting demands and new exploration and development of oil and gas fields and plays. This flexibility would be especially useful in the future for allocating funds to coordinate and process use authorizations in those offices where industry forecasts increased development of oil and gas resources and the BLM offices had not previously been identified as project offices. For example, in FY 2013, the Pinedale Field Office in Wyoming received 383 APDs; the Bakersfield Field Office in California received 212 APDs; and the White River Field Office in Colorado, received 198 APDs. Although these offices have received high volumes of drilling permit applications in recent years, none were previously designated as pilot project offices under the EPAct because they were not experiencing such extensive development at the time of the bill's enactment. In contrast, the Rawlins Field Office, identified as a pilot office in the EPAct, only received 42 permit applications during FY 2013.

The continuation of the program provided by S. 2440 will also support our partner agencies, such as the U.S. Fish and Wildlife Service, the Bureau of Indian Affairs, the U.S. Forest Service, the Environmental Protection Agency, the Army Corps of Engineers, and the appropriate State government offices, in devoting staff to the increased workload in these new areas. This coordination with our partner agencies is a crucial part of the BLM's success in this program.

The BLM also welcomes the bill's establishment of a $9,500 APD processing fee indexed for inflation through 2026. This is an increase from the $6,500 fee that the Congress has implemented through annual appropriations and the increased fee more closely reflects the true average cost of processing APDs on the Federal and Indian Trust mineral estate. This fee is an important component of the funding for the BLM's permitting program and will allow the BLM to continue to process permits and maintain a robust onshore oil and gas permitting program. The BLM does not, however, support the bill's prohibition of the Secretary from implementing a rulemaking that would enable an increase in fees to recover additional costs from industry related to processing its applications for permits to drill. While not currently envisioned, the BLM would like to maintain the option of designing a fee system that reflects the varying costs associated with different APDs. This would be barred under the existing and proposed moratorium.

Finally, the Administration has generally not supported the extension of the special pilot office funding rental receipts, as rental receipts are not strongly correlated to program funding needs and diverting these revenues from the Treasury would require spending offsets elsewhere. Instead, we have proposed that program operating funds come from a combination of user fees and regular discretionary appropriations. However, if the Committee wishes to continue this rental receipts approach, BLM recommends that the bill be amended to increase BLM's flexibility in how and where the funds are spent. In particular, we recommend clarifying that the permit processing funds may be made available for the processing and coordination of oil and gas use authorizations for both Federal and Indian Trust oil and gas assets.

Conclusion

The BLM supports the goals of S. 2440 and looks forward to working with the Committee on technical and clarifying modifications to the bill. Thank you for the opportunity to provide testimony on S. 2440.

ON S. 279

Thank you for the opportunity to present the views of the Department of the Interior on S. 279, the Public Land Renewable Energy Development Act of 2013. The legislation seeks to expedite the development of geothermal, wind, and solar energy projects on Federal lands managed by the Departments of the Interior, Agriculture, and Defense. This statement addresses the provisions relevant to the Department of the Interior (Department).

The Department and the Bureau of Land Management (BLM) are committed to responsibly mobilizing the tremendous renewable energy resources available on public lands, and share the Committee's interest in identifying efficiencies in the development of those resources, consistent with environmental protection and public involvement in agency decision-making. The Department supports the goals of S. 279, and would like to work with the sponsor and the Committee on our shared objective of furthering geothermal, wind, and solar energy development while continuing to protect our nation's public land and water resources.

Renewable Energy Development on Public Lands

As part of the Administration's "All-of-the-Above" energy strategy, the Department has made the development of the New Energy Frontier on America's public lands one of its top priorities. Due in large part to a permitting process for renewable energy projects emphasizing early consultation with partners and stakeholders, in 2012, the BLM successfully accomplished the Energy Policy Act of 2005 (EPAct) goal of authorizing over 10,000 megawatts (MWs) of renewable energy on public lands—three years ahead of schedule. In support of the President's Climate Action Plan to ensure America's continued leadership in clean energy, the Department is now working to reach 20,000 MWs of permitted renewable energy capacity on public lands by 2020. The BLM is already making great strides toward achieving that goal, which would provide enough clean energy to power more than 6 million homes.

In 2009, there were no commercial solar energy projects on or under development on public lands. Since that time, the BLM has approved 52 renewable energy projects; including 29 utility-scale solar facilities, 11 wind farms, and 12 geothermal plants, each with associated transmission corridors and infrastructure to connect with established power grids. If fully built, these projects will provide more than 14,000 MWs of power, which will and support approximately 21,000 construction and operations jobs.

The BLM recently announced it will prioritize 13 renewable energy projects (11 solar and two wind) that it will focus on in 2014 and 2015. The 13 projects represent approximately 3,030 MWs in potential clean energy. The recent successful auction of solar energy leases in the Dry Lake Solar Energy Zone in Nevada is also likely to result in additional projects and increased generation.

Renewable energy projects authorized by the BLM constitute a major contribution to not only the nation's energy grid, but also the national economy. Projects on public lands have already garnered an estimated $8.6 billion in total capital investments, and the potential for approved projects pending construction is estimated at $28 billion. Through efficient and environmentally-responsible permitting, the BLM is helping to bring tens of billions of dollars in investments to the United States.

The BLM intends to further these contributions by moving from an application-by-application approach for solar energy projects to a competitive leasing process in designated development areas called Solar Energy Zones (SEZs). In October 2012, the Department finalized a Solar Energy Programmatic Environmental Impact Statement, more commonly called the Western Solar Plan, which identified 17 SEZs and established a blueprint for utility-scale solar energy permitting with access to existing or planned transmission infrastructure. The Western Solar Plan also provides the foundation for the BLM's current rulemaking process to implement competitive solar and wind energy leasing within designated areas.

In authorizing existing projects, reviewing proposed projects, and developing a competitive leasing rule, the BLM has focused on managing renewable energy development in an accelerated but responsible manner which ensures the protection of signature landscapes, wildlife habitats, and cultural resources. This "smart from the start" approach is consistent with the Administration's goal of authorizing safe and sustainable geothermal, wind, and solar energy projects on public lands. The BLM achieves these collaborative goals through close working relationships with local communities, state regulators, private industry, and other Federal agencies.

Under land use plans and environmental analyses informed by public involvement and early consultation with these partners, the BLM is leading the nation toward the New Energy Frontier through active geothermal, wind, and solar energy programs.

S. 279, Public Land Renewable Energy Development Act of 2013

S. 279 aims to increase renewable energy development on public lands, primarily through the reestablishment of a special account for processing geothermal energy authorizations and the creation of a competitive wind and solar leasing pilot program. The bill would also establish a royalty system for wind and solar energy authorizations, create a conservation fund to address some of the impacts of wind and solar energy development on public lands, and require the Secretary of the Interior and of Agriculture to determine the feasibility of carrying out a conservation banking program. The bill's provisions are directed toward all public and National Forest System lands that have not been excluded from solar or wind energy development by a land use plan, Resource Management Plan, or Federal law.

The bill would also require the Secretary of Agriculture and of Defense to separately analyze potential renewable energy development impacts and opportunities on the respective lands they manage. The Department of the Interior and Department of Defense would need to coordinate on the review of public lands withdrawn for military purposes to ensure that any development would be congruent with existing authorities, current military needs, as well as long-term public interests.

Since this bill and previous versions were introduced, the Department has utilized administrative authorities to implement the Western Solar Plan and expand solar, wind, and geothermal development opportunities on public lands. The Department supports the goals of S. 279, and we are excited to work with the Committee and the sponsor to further harness the vast renewable resources on public lands while continuing to ensure a fair return to U.S. taxpayers.

S. 279 would amend the Energy Policy Act of 2005 to reestablish the geothermal special account, which expired in 2010, through Fiscal Year 2020 to provide funds for the processing of geothermal leases and use authorizations. Under current law, 50 percent of geothermal revenues are directed to the state in which the project is located, with the remaining funds divided evenly between the county in which the project is located and the Treasury. Under S. 279, the states would continue to receive 50 percent of geothermal revenues; while the BLM would receive an amount subject to appropriation and without fiscal year limitation from the total directed to the Treasury. The BLM estimates the proposed special account would generate $4 million per year in funding for the program, which is currently supported by $7 million in appropriated funds. The Department has generally proposed funding geothermal program operations through a combination of cost recovery fees and the regular appropriations process. We look forward to working with this Committee and the Interior appropriations committees in evaluating funding options for the geothermal leasing program.

Section 203 of S. 279 would establish a pilot program for the competitive leasing of wind and solar energy sites on Federal lands. The bill requires the pilot program be established within 180 days of enactment and expanded to all covered lands within two years of enactment following a joint determination by the Secretaries of the Interior and of Agriculture. Under the proposed pilot program, the Secretary would select two solar and wind project sites within 90 days of the program's establishment to be made available for development through competitive leasing. The section also outlines various competitive leasing requirements, including the payment of royalties, fees, and bonuses; lease terms and readjustments; and the issuance of regulations for reclamation and restoration bonding requirements.

The Department shares goals similar to those of Section 203, and through its existing authorities, is currently developing a competitive leasing program for solar and wind energy projects on public lands. In 2012, the BLM completed its Western Solar Plan which designated 17 Solar Energy Zones (SEZs) and included the decision to proceed with competitive leasing for solar projects in those areas. The BLM recently completed a successful competitive leasing auction in the Dry Lake SEZ in Nevada, which resulted in $5.8 million in high bids. The BLM plans to build on the success of the Dry Lake auction, and anticipates publishing a proposed competitive leasing rule by the end of 2014. This rule will give additional detail to the competitive leasing program for the solar and wind energy programs. The BLM's current rulemaking process reflects the goals of S. 279 in implementing a competitive leasing process, and the agency would like to work with the sponsor and the Committee on improvements to the proposed language.

The Department also shares the legislation's goal of capturing the fair market value of leased projects as part of its commitment to ensure an appropriate return to U.S. taxpayers. While the BLM currently ensures a fair return to the public from solar and wind energy authorizations through an annual acreage rent and MW capacity fee, the agency is also supportive of efforts which could improve and simplify how that return is captured. The Department is glad to work with the sponsor and the Committee on exploring alternative ways to secure an appropriate return to taxpayers from solar and wind projects' use of public lands.

The Department is concerned, however, that the royalty system proposed under S. 279 would not provide a fair return from projects during periods without electric generation. We recommend the Committee augment the legislation to include a revenue collection system covering all phases of project development and operation.

Section 206 of S. 279 would require the development of a comprehensive inspection, collection, fiscal, and production accounting and auditing system by the BLM and Department's Office of Natural Resources Revenue. Replacing the existing annual acreage and MW capacity fee with the system necessary to accurately determine royalties would require the Department to collect, track, and audit significantly different types of information from what is currently collected. The Department would need additional time and resources to develop a robust royalty auditing system capable of ensuring a fair return. The Department looks forward to working with Committee to determine the best way to meet the revenue capturing objectives of the legislation.

Section 204 of S. 279 provides for the allocation of royalty and bonus revenues from solar and wind energy leases to states (25 percent), counties (25 percent), a Renewable Energy Resource Conservation Fund (35 percent), and the Treasury (15 percent). Under the bill, funds deposited in the Treasury are to be directed to the BLM or other Federal or state agencies to assist in the processing of renewable energy permits for 15 years, after which the 15 percent of total revenue from solar and wind authorizations would be redirected to the Conservation Fund. Currently all such revenues from solar and wind energy authorizations on public lands go to the Treasury.

Finally, section 210 of the bill would revoke the rental fee exemptions provided under the Rural Electrification Act (REA) for solar and wind projects with a capacity of 20 MWs or more. While the BLM has not yet approved any eligible projects under the REA, future projects may qualify for rental exemptions under existing authorities. The BLM supports the removal of the rental fee exemption as provided under S. 279.

Conclusion

Facilitating the responsible development of renewable energy resources on public lands remains a cornerstone of the Administration's broad energy strategy. The Department and BLM both support efforts to safely advance geothermal exploration and renewable energy opportunities on public lands, and we look forward to working with the Committee and sponsors of the legislation on these shared goals.

The CHAIR. Thank you, Mr. Kornze.

Listening in the reading in your testimony you would, I guess, you would think that there were no problems that either the Democrats or the Republicans on this committee have pointed out in their opening statements. I'm just having a hard time, kind of, understanding the tenor or tone, as well as some of the issues that you raised in your opening statement.

Tell me again what percentage of the land you have under management for oil and gas production? What's your total acreage is and how much you have under lease?

Mr. KORNZE. So the Bureau of Land Management manages about 245 million acres, about 36 million acres is currently leased.

The CHAIR. So 36 million acres is a small percentage of 245. Not that, I mean, significant, but I mean, still a relatively small percentage.

No. 2, how many permits have you issued in the last 4 years for solar production on BLM land?

Mr. KORNZE. About 29, I believe is the number.

The CHAIR. Twenty-nine permits. There are 29 projects under construction?

Mr. KORNZE. There are, I believe, I could get the exact numbers, but I would say about 15 of the projects have been built among the 52 renewable energy projects we've authorized and about another——

The CHAIR. On public land.

Mr. KORNZE. About another 10 are under construction.

The CHAIR. OK.

Mr. KORNZE. Yes.

The CHAIR. Then go through those production numbers again because I'm just having a hard time figuring out whether we are producing more, producing less, producing the same. So go ahead and give that testimony again about the amount of production on Federal land from oil and gas?

Mr. KORNZE. So when it comes to oil the numbers are up.

The CHAIR. Up?

Mr. KORNZE. We're at a 10-year high.

The CHAIR. OK.

On public land.

Mr. KORNZE. On public land, 7 percent up from last year, about 30 percent up since the beginning of the Administration.

The CHAIR. Do you have the volumes that you can testify to?

Mr. KORNZE. I can provide those to the committee.

The CHAIR. OK. By barrels.

Mr. KORNZE. Sure.

The CHAIR. Then what about natural gas?

Mr. KORNZE. When it comes to natural gas, natural gas is down.

The CHAIR. By what percentage? Over what time period?

Mr. KORNZE. I'll find that before you before we're done talking.

The CHAIR. OK. If you could give, I think, an outlook for 10 years is helpful so we're, you know, trying to be fair in our analysis and not pick the high year or the low year.

Mr. KORNZE. Yes.

The CHAIR. So over the last ten.

Part of the reason we called this hearing and these bills have been introduced is because the IG report says that some of these permits are waiting more than, I think that they said, an average and at least in the testimony that I saw, an average of 200 days.

Do you dispute that or are you agreeing with that?

Mr. KORNZE. So let me give you some natural gas information and then I'll go to the permitting.

Natural gas is down 9 percent from last year and down 12 percent since 2008. We can get you a 10-year figure.

The CHAIR. If you could get a 10-year that would be terrific.

Mr. KORNZE. You bet.

So when it comes to permitting in 2011 our average was over 300 days. Two years ago it was 225 days. Last year it was 196.

The CHAIR. But doesn't the law require a 30-day turn around?

Mr. KORNZE. The law asks us that within 30 days we make a decision as to whether or not to approve, deny or indicate that more evaluation is needed. So there is a roughly a 30-day goal, but it is not rigid.

The CHAIR. So there are maybe 95 percent of your reviews have resulted in more information is needed within that 30-day.

Mr. KORNZE. Many do, yes.

The CHAIR. Can you, after, maybe just by your preparation for this meeting, give this committee categories of some of the types of permits that are falling into that need more information. Either people aren't knowing exactly or companies aren't having enough detail about what you're looking for. So they're either not receiving it correctly or you're not giving it out correctly.

There's got to be some issue that that percentage of applications would fall into the need more information category. I mean, these are pretty experienced drillers, not a lot of fly by night operators that come in. I mean, you've got to have some standing to do this work.

So could you provide our committee with a little deeper analysis of that so that we could help you figure out how to get better in compliance with what, I think, this committee wants to do which is clear, transparent, relatively short, comprehensive, not, you know, skimping on the review in any way, for the benefit of multiple land use. But I think those numbers, 300-day delays, are pretty shocking, at least to me.

Mr. KORNZE. Yes.

The CHAIR. Senator, I have a few other questions. I want to turn that over to you though now and we'll go through a round of questioning.

Senator MURKOWSKI. Great. Thank you.

Madame Chairman, I think it's very important the questions that you're asking in trying to really distill these numbers here. I want to make sure that we're comparing apples to apples here because as I understand it back in June when EIA released this report on Federal and Indian lands. Again, this was over the past 10 years.

They say that coal production is down 8 percent.

Crude oil and lease condensate production are down 11 percent.

Natural gas production is down 43 percent.

So overall, over the past decade, fossil fuel production from Federal and Indian lands declined by 21.2 percent overall.

Now some of the smart guys back behind me are saying well, maybe your figures aren't counting the subsurface mineral estate. I want to make sure that we're all counting the same way because it's real easy to throw numbers around here. I want to really try to understand exactly what we're talking about here.

So if we can drill down into that. Ha Ha Ha.

[Laughter.]

Senator MURKOWSKI. I would appreciate it.

Sorry.

The CHAIR. No pun intended.

Senator MURKOWSKI. I can't help myself.

Mr. Kornze, I wanted to ask you a couple questions on the status of things in the NPRA. The President keeps talking about oil and gas development up in NPRA as part of the all of the above, but really beyond holding lease sales I'm not really seeing much that's being done by the Administration to ensure that project in the petroleum reserve can be successfully developed.

Greater Mooses Tooth 1 is the project that we're following very, very closely right now. It's going to be the first production in NPRA, expected to add 30,000 barrels of oil per day to TAPS. Of course, given what we're seeing with the 5 and 6 percent decline in TAPS, this is really critical that we get online.

So we've got a couple issues with regards to the timing here.

I'm concerned that the date for the release of the final supplemental EIS is going to slip. As I understand that timeline now, the EIS must be released in October to allow the Corps to begin the processing here of the 404 permit to allow road construction for the winter.

Already we've got 120-day minimum review period for the Corps. This would push a 404 permit to January.

So the problem is if this EIS slips any further this construction season is going to be lost and the project delayed for yet another year which, in my view, is absolutely unacceptable.

So the question to you this afternoon is does the BLM plan to issue the final supplemental EIS by October so that we can get this project moving forward in 2015?

Mr. KORNZE. So I appreciate you raising this. The National Petroleum Reserve is an incredible resource for the country. We are working expeditiously through that process right now. We're also in conversation with, in order to get to a final EIS, to make sure that there are answers and more information for the public to evaluate.

We're also in conversation with the Army Corps of Engineers to see if they can get started on their review independently. We've seen some favorable indications that they might be able to start soon.

So I'm optimistic that the timelines will work out.

Senator MURKOWSKI. So you think you can stick to this timeline so that everything that needs to happen in order to begin work in 2015 can commence?

Mr. KORNZE. We are headed in that direction.

Senator MURKOWSKI. OK.

One of the concerns that we're hearing, of course, is that BLM may proceed with only approving GMT 1 as a road less project which would make the project just uneconomic. So can you commit to me that BLM will not proceed with a road less or even a seasonally road less alternative?

Mr. KORNZE. So one of our alternatives does include road less analysis. That's something that we are looking and going to have to evaluate as we evaluate all the alternatives.

Senator MURKOWSKI. But would you agree that if you take that approach and you go road less or even seasonally road less, what that does to the economics of this project?

Mr. KORNZE. We will pay close attention to the viability of the project with whatever option is ultimately chosen.

Senator MURKOWSKI. You know, this is a project that is supported as a roaded development by both the regional and the native village corporation, both ASRC and Kuukpik Corporation. The locals have come out strongly in favor of the proposal. Without road access the reality is is the only alternative that is available then is by aircraft which, of course, puts greater stress on the caribou as they are traveling around, greater stress on the subsistence hunting.

So I want to make sure. I know that you've been up there. But I want to make sure that you are aware of the very high level of local support for a road to GMT 1.

Mr. KORNZE. Yes, I certainly am. I did greatly appreciate the opportunity to get up there in February. I think it was about 40 below that day. We went out to see the sites.

Senator MURKOWSKI. Nice day?

Mr. KORNZE. It was beautiful.

We also had a community meeting in Nuiqsut where folks expressed, very clearly, the same sentiment that you have shared.

Senator MURKOWSKI. I appreciate that you went up there. I guess I would just, again, reinforce the timeliness of these decisions is absolutely key because if we lose yet another season. Again, that goes to the economics of a project. Then if the option is road less or seasonally road less, I think it just kills it which again, would not be in keeping with this Administration's mantra that they support an all of the above policy.

Thank you, Madame Chairman.

The CHAIR. Thank you.

Senator Heinrich.

Senator HEINRICH. Thank you, Chair Landrieu and thank you for holding this timely hearing.

I thought I'd start and just by point a few things out simply because I appreciate the effort by the Chair and Ranking Member to, sort of, try and get at some apples to apples comparisons.

In New Mexico oil production is up. We're at 46 million barrels last year. The No. 1, western producer on Federal land, I believe, at the moment.

But at the same time natural gas is down.

Those are very much tied to, in large part, commodity prices. Price plays a real role as to whether or not something is going to be produced or not. The depression in natural gas prices has meant there has been places that are very viable under different price arrangements that are simply not being produced today.

However, given the stability in the oil market, that relative high price, we have seen that very successful in the last few years.

I'd also just point out in terms of the percentage leased, at least from my point of view in the State of New Mexico, the leasing is largely going to be focused in places where there's actually oil and gas. So within the San Juan Basin on BLM land within the Permian Basin on BLM land and basins that may be developed in the future, you see a lot of leasing going on.

In the Southwest part of the State, for example, there's a good deal of BLM land that you're not going to see a lot of leasing in simply because there's no resource there or it hasn't been discovered if there is.

I want to ask Director Kornze, I think, by all accounts from everybody you've heard from the pilot process—the pilot offices have been incredibly successful in promoting oil and gas development on both Federal and tribal lands. With the authorization expiring next year are you starting to see an impact of that uncertainty in future funding, in terms of the Bureau of Land Management's ability to fill staff vacancies?

Mr. KORNZE. I appreciate that question.

The short answer is yes. We are seeing some uncertainty in the hiring process because we want to be able to offer folks some long term view of sustainability of their positions with that authorization expiring next year. We have over 200 positions within the Bureau of Land Management that have a question mark around them.

So it matters to those teams. Last week or the week before, I was in Silt, Colorado at one of our pilot offices. They were able to double the size of their team with this funding. So half of that office is focused and funded through this authorization. So it makes a difference for sure.

Senator HEINRICH. Great.

About what fraction of the BLM's staff in New Mexico State office are funded under the pilot program? Do you know?

Mr. KORNZE. So I believe we have about 650 BLM employees in New Mexico and about 10 percent of those, I think, would be an appropriate number that would funded through this program.

Senator HEINRICH. With the main original pilot program is Carlsbad office, are those employees able to focus on leasing demand anywhere in the State? In other words if, you know, if demand surges in the San Juan Basin verses the Permian Basin are they able to help with, balance that out over time?

Mr. KORNZE. It does get complicated in terms of what kind of funding we put behind various activities. So we can often find a way to make that work, but having the flexibility that's built into this new version.

Senator HEINRICH. Yes.

Mr. KORNZE. Is going to make our lives and those authorizations easier.

Senator HEINRICH. That's very helpful.

Under existing law, Director Kornze, where do the revenues from renewable energy projects on Federal lands used for and are any of those revenues retained by the BLM to cover the cost of just doing the permitting?

Mr. KORNZE. Yup.

So all the revenues we collect from renewable energy projects go back to the Treasury.

Senator HEINRICH. So none of it can be used to pay for the overhead that is required to actually permit those—or those projects?

Mr. KORNZE. No.

Senator HEINRICH. If the BLM did have dedicated funding to cover administrative costs what impact do you think that would have on your ability to offer leases and process permits in a more timely manner?

Mr. KORNZE. The ability to have some sustained funding would allow us, not unlike in the oil and gas realm, to have some sustained, well trained, well experienced teams that we could put together that could help really drive this because when you put new folks on a project, just like in any situation, it takes a while to come up to speed.

Senator HEINRICH. Since the completion of the solar energy zones in 2012 how many of those zones have an active auction or application process?

Mr. KORNZE. We've had two auctions. At this point we actually don't. We need a rule which we're working on to give us leasing authority within those zones, competitive leasing authority.

But right now if we do see multiple applications within a zone we can go through a very—it's almost like a competitive process.

Senator HEINRICH. Thank you very much.

Madame Chair.

The CHAIR. Thank you.

I think it's Senator Portman and then Senator Risch? I'm sorry, Senator Risch. I'm sorry, I like to depend on the staff.

Senator Portman.

Senator PORTMAN. Thank you, Madame Chair.

You know, I snuck in earlier on you, Jim, sorry.

Senator RISCH. You got off the elevator ahead of me. You elbowed me back.

Senator PORTMAN. Yes.

[Laughter.]

Senator RISCH. As usual.

Senator PORTMAN. I snuck over earlier today and I made some comments already on this, but Mr. Kornze what I want to talk about is the general issue of permitting. I do think these two bills we have before us make sense. I congratulate those on the committee who moved these forward.

But we've got a bigger problem in this country. Under our current permitting system, including for energy projects, we take so much time that investors often tend to leave and go elsewhere including overseas to make their investments. I mentioned earlier that there is a study by the IMF saying we're 17th in the world in terms of green lighting a project.

The World Bank has its own ease of doing business study and they show we're now 34th in the world in terms of countries dealing with the requirements of permitting.

By the way, we were 30th last year. So we're going in the wrong direction.

What I hear from people and I heard this in Ohio initially from actually some folks trying to put hydro on the Ohio River, believe it or not, is, you know, it's just impossible to wait the 5, 6, 7 years sometimes it takes so these investors are going somewhere else.

We have legislation to deal with this. It's broader that would deal with BLM lands and other public lands, but also deals with this broader issue. You may be familiar with it.

If you are, I'd love to have your opinion on it. But it's called the Federal Permitting Improvement Act. Senator McCaskill and I are the authors of it. We have 7 Democrats on board now including the Chair, Senator Landrieu. I appreciate that support. Senator Manchin and others, Senator Barrasso is one of the original co-sponsors.

It just makes sense. It basically says let's take all these recommendations from the President's Jobs Council from business round table, chamber of commerce and others and try to put them to work to better coordinate the Federal permitting process to set some deadlines. There's testimony recently before the Subcommittee on Energy and Power in the House saying that there could be as many as 35 separate Federal permits required for a single energy project. That's part of the problem that requires the coordination.

We also, though, set up better transparency, more stakeholder participation earlier. We just, like, litigation delays, as you probably know. That's one of the huge issues that reduces the statute of limitations from 6 years to 150 days.

I just think we need this desperately if we're going to be able to get on track for more investment and move forward, including taking advantage of these great resources we have in this country and getting some of this permitting done.

I would ask you about your process, you know, through the preparation of this hearing been hearing some about some of the timeframes being longer timeframes than on private lands, obviously, but when you're processing an energy permit for a project on BLM land, does BLM have an institutionalized process for consulting with the other Federal agencies?

Mr. KORNZE. It's been a big focus over the last 4 or 5 years to increase those early conversations in coordination with other agencies.

I should say, off the top, that getting to an answer, a no, a yes, is important, right? So we acknowledge that. We share that, that vision, that having, you know, evaluations that go on for years and years and years doesn't provide the certainty and the type of back and forth that is more productive.

So when it comes to renewable energy one of the ways that we've helped stand up that program, it was through some very aggressive coordination between agencies because, frankly, there was very, very little, just miniscule renewable energy that had been authorized on public lands prior to this Administration. So that's been a focus.

One of the things that we——

Senator PORTMAN. That includes some of the renewable projects you've done in California where you fast tracked them?

Mr. KORNZE. It does.

Senator PORTMAN. Are those same fast track procedures effective with regard to other renewables wind, say, and with regard to oil and gas?

Mr. KORNZE. Yes. The same teams are working on those projects.

Senator PORTMAN. Are you using those for oil and gas production, for instance, in other States?

Mr. KORNZE. We are. So that was my next point is that what this program from the Energy Policy Act has allowed us to do is to actually help pay for individuals from other agencies to work with us, so Fish and Wildlife Service, the Army Corps of Engineers, State Historical Preservation Officer.

We use some of the funding for BLM employees. We also use some of that funding to pay other agencies to bring employees to the table and to work with us on clearances.

Senator PORTMAN. Do you have a lead agency in that case? Is it you?

Mr. KORNZE. In these energy authorizations we're talking about, yes, we would be the lead.

Senator PORTMAN. Do you have dashboard, you know, the transparency that's been talked about in our bill and other recommendations where people can find out what the process is, how long it's taking, what the hold ups are?

Is there some transparency there for stakeholders?

Mr. KORNZE. We provide annual numbers and most project proponents have a very close relationship with the office that they're working through. So they would have a fair amount of insight into what's happening.

Senator PORTMAN. When another Federal agent says it wants to review a permit how does BLM notify the project sponsor about that?

Let's say a Federal agency steps in and says, hey, I'd like to have my own review here. Do you have a way to notify the project sponsors?

Mr. KORNZE. So we coordinate with Federal agencies all the time. So we stay in close touch with project proponents and let them know, you know, what step we're at, which—it's no surprise to folks working on major projects that the various agencies will come to the table. Often we will hold an initial pre-application meeting that will have all the relevant agencies might even come to the table.

Senator PORTMAN. My time has expired. Governor Risch is here and he's got to run too.

But I just, if you could take a look at this legislation, this broader legislation, and give us your opinion. That would be very helpful given you know a lot about permitting now and, you know, again, this doesn't relate solely to public lands much less BLM lands. But we would like your input on it.

Again, this is legislation that's bipartisan, that meets some of the requirements that the President's own advisors through the President's Business Council have recommended.

We'd appreciate your input on the Federal Permitting Improvement Act.

Mr. KORNZE. Thank you, Senator.

One thing I would like to add in is that, so, we have made some improvements in our APD, our drilling permit processing recently, similar to the dashboard you mentioned. We are looking to pilot and then fully implement next year an online permitting system that will—right now we're using paper to go back and forth between drillers and ourselves. It's horribly inefficient, as you can imagine.

So we have at least one office that's using an online system. Their numbers are half of our national numbers in terms of time. So we think there's huge efficiencies that can be had.

Part of it is that an application is incomplete which happens very often. So Carlsbad, New Mexico which is the office I'm talking about that has a system in place that they designed locally. One out of 12, excuse me, only 1 out of 12 applications that comes into them for drilling is complete on the first instance.

The other 11 require a significant amount of back and forth.

So having an online system where there is some transparency and some ability for the project proponent to know what more is needed on a very quick basis is something that we're headed toward and we're excited about.

Senator PORTMAN. Good. That sounds positive. Thank you.

Thank you, Madame Chair.

The CHAIR. Thank you for raising those important issues.

Senator Barrasso. I'm sorry, Senator Risch.

Senator RISCH. Thank you, Madame Chairman.

Mr. Kornze, thank you for what you do.

There's a lot of people in America don't understand in States like the one I live in and other Western States, the tremendous reach of the Federal Government with the number of acres that it has, but more importantly the conflict between people who want to use or don't want to use those lands. Your job is to reconcile those.

It's not an easy job. I understand that.

The title of this hearing is Breaking the Logjam. So I want to talk to you about one of the logs. On May 7th I wrote a letter to the Secretary along with Senator Crapo, along with our two Congressman. It had to do with the proposed Boardman to Hemmingway transmission line.

I don't know how familiar you are with that particular project. But I want to underscore to you, first of all, it's been since May 7th and we haven't heard back. That particular transmission project, the proposed date for the draft EIS, was in November 2012. We still haven't seen the draft.

So finally I asked is this one of the draft EIS. It's been delayed for 6 times.

Now I understand, of course, there's issues with the sage grouse and everything else with as is usual with these. I'd like to know when we're going to get a response to our letter. But you can forget about that if you can tell me when the draft EIS is going to come out.

Can you shed any light on that for us?

Mr. KORNZE. OK. So this is a project I'm aware of. I can't tell you when the draft is going to come out. I can check on that and we can give your team a call.

Senator RISCH. I would appreciate that.

Mr. KORNZE. But we'll get that letter to you next week.

Senator RISCH. Thank you.

Mr. KORNZE. Share that information.

Senator RISCH. That's good service. I appreciate that.

Mr. KORNZE. OK.

Senator RISCH. We'd like to see it. Even more importantly we'd like to see the draft EIS.

Mr. KORNZE. Yes.

Senator RISCH. I know it's on the radar screen at BLM and it's important to us out there.

So, thank you very much.

Mr. KORNZE. You bet.

That is one project where I'll share that, you know, I think there's some steps along the way where we could have been more efficient to date. I've talked to my team about that.

Also though, I think, we've had somewhat of slow response from the proponent on a few occasions. I think we're trying to work through that and hopefully the rest of the process will be much smoother.

Senator RISCH. Thanks, Mr. Kornze. That's good.

Thank you, Madame Chair.

The CHAIR. Thank you.

I think we're ready to move to the second panel. But before we do let me just get something into the record. The estimates that we went over initially was that BLM currently has 3,500 applications for permits for drilling that are backlogged. I think we're having some difficulty finding out what offices have the most pending of these permits.

Do you all have that breakdown by office?

I'm looking at a document that I'm going to submit for the record here that has, for instance.

An Alaska total of 5 applications for permits to drill.

But wells that have not been drilled in California, the total is 177.

Colorado, 544.

New Mexico, 1,337.

Utah, 1,769.

Then the big State, Wyoming, 2,446.

So these are permits that have been granted, but wells that have not been drilled. That's one piece of information that's important.

But what we really wanted the breakdown of backlogs by office. Do you have that you can send to us?

Mr. KORNZE. We sure do. We can get that to you.

The CHAIR. OK. Could you give us, for the record, what is the leading office, the highest number of backlogs, what office is that?

Mr. KORNZE. Yes.

Vernal has the great—Vernal, Utah.

The CHAIR. OK. How many are pending or backlogged?

What is the backlog, the number?

Mr. KORNZE. So there's a few numbers here that's important to parse out for what they mean, how BLM talks about them. So see if that's helpful to you.

So we consider active applications. So we've got about 3,500 active applications which we're working on.

We consider that we've got about a thousand of those that are in the backlog category which means that they've been with us for 90 days and that they're complete because only about a third of those 3,500 applications that we're working on are complete.

So we're still going back and forth with the applicant.

Vernal has——

The CHAIR. You may not call them a backlog, but I think that many members of this committee would call the whole 3,500 a backlog.

Mr. KORNZE. Yes.

The CHAIR. I'm having a very hard time really understanding for in—and we'll hear from the second panel, I think, more about this. This is not a new phenomena drilling or developing Federal land. It's been going on for decades.

These companies are very, very familiar. So I'm just having a hard time understanding how so many of these applications can be incomplete when they come to you. What is the incompleteness, the nature of it. Is it a date that's not, a signature that's missing or is it a whole section of description of their project?

I'm really going to drill down and find out because, you know, it just doesn't sound efficient to me that two thirds of the applications would come in would not be complete. I'd say 90 percent of them should be complete. Ten percent, I mean, that would be what you'd roughly think, 10 percent of the people aren't paying attention. They're not really following the rules, but not, you know, that large a number.

Then how quickly you can get them complete.

But give us the office that has the most backlog and what it is under your definition of backlog.

Mr. KORNZE. So it's still Vernal, Utah.

But, so and I can appreciate the view you provide on that 3,500 being——

The CHAIR. We'll drill down a little bit, but let's talk about Utah.

Mr. KORNZE. We're working through.

But I think it's also important to lay over that that the BLM process is, on average, between 4 and 5,000 drilling permits each year. So that 3,500, we're actually doing what comes in the door and doing more. So we're working down that backlog list and getting better in the last number of years.

We also have 7,000 drilling permits that are out there and available to use that have been authorized in the last few years.

So, I think, I can understand the desire for efficiency. We share it. But I do think we also have a positive story to tell in terms of the improvements we've made largely under the efforts that have been made possible through the Energy Policy Act and the special program that we're talking about today.

The CHAIR. OK, that's fair. But what is the pending number in the office in Utah?

Mr. KORNZE. So there's about, in our category of backlog, there's about 900 that are in backlog.

The CHAIR. In that one office?

Mr. KORNZE. Out of about 1,050. That's because those APD applications come in and they basically with the understanding of the proponents they've been put to the side while a large EIS for a huge field is being developed. So there's two very large EISs taking place.

Once those EISs are completed and we've done other big ones in Utah, like Gasco and West Tavaputs, those APDs just start rolling through.

The CHAIR. Rolling.

Mr. KORNZE. Very, very quickly.

The CHAIR. OK.

Mr. KORNZE. So our Vernal office is our highest producer. Those folks, they're very good at what they do.

The CHAIR. I understand that.

Go right ahead and then we'll move to the second panel.

Senator MURKOWSKI. Very quick follow on then.

So with these permits that are part of this backlog, these pending permits have a 2-year life to their permit. What consideration then is being made to extending for an additional 2 years, if you've got all this stuff that is then sitting in a backlog process?

Mr. KORNZE. So there is a provision. It used to be they were good for 1 year and you could extend for 1 year. The Energy Policy Act made it good for 2 years. You can extend for 2 years.

So folks have to come in. Talk to our offices. I think our offices are usually fairly kind in terms of providing an extension of that.

Senator MURKOWSKI. But you only have a one extension.

Mr. KORNZE. Yes.

Senator MURKOWSKI. So if you have a continued backlog that continues for a period of years you may run your first permit period and then your extension that is allowed. Then what happens? You're out of luck?

Mr. KORNZE. At that point in your application, well, are you thinking? So are you thinking that this EIS is taking place and what do you do?

Senator MURKOWSKI. I'm assuming the EIS is taking place is what you had said.

Mr. KORNZE. Yes. So in this case in Vernal so that the applications haven't been processed, so therefore it's that the clock hasn't started.

Senator MURKOWSKI. OK.

Mr. KORNZE. On the permit and that 2- to 4-year period. That would only start after the APD is issued.

Senator MURKOWSKI. But once it's issued you have one opportunity for a 2-year extension?

Mr. KORNZE. Yes. But it would be issued, the NEPA would be completed and you would be just fine to go out and start drilling. Right?

So once you have that APD you have the authority to go.

It's not that the larger EISs are holding up APDs that have been issued.

Senator MURKOWSKI. OK.

The CHAIR. Excellent questions.

Let's move to our second panel.

I hope, Director, that you can stay, if your schedule would permit to listen to this panel of local and State experts. They've traveled a long way to come give their testimony. We'd appreciate it if you could hear them.

Thank you very much.

Mr. KORNZE. Yes.

The CHAIR. As you all come forward I'll introduce you. We're going to try to finish up by, you know, by 4:30 if we can.

Mr. Scott Kidwell, Director of Government Affairs for Concho Resources. Mr. Kidwell has a background in regulatory affairs.

Ms. Kathleen Sgamma representing Western Energy Alliance where she serves as the Vice President of Government and Public Affairs.

Commissioner Mark Christensen, Chairman of Campbell County Board of Commissioners from Wyoming, Gillette, Wyoming. He's here on behalf of the Wyoming County Commissioner Association, representing 23 counties.

We have Commissioner Lorinda Wichman, Vice Chair of Nye County Commission in Nevada. She's also President-Elect of Nevada Association of Counties.

Mr. Arthur Haubenstock, Solar Energy Industry, he's an attorney that focuses on private and public sector experience in utility placement.

Then we finally have Mr. Scott Nichols, who is here representing U.S. Geothermal, Inc., Permitting Lands Manager. He has a good deal of experience in geothermal, environmental data, mining and distribution.

Senator Risch wanted to introduce, say a special word about one of our witnesses and say a word and then he's going to have to leave.

We'll look forward to having all of your testimony.

Senator RISCH. Madame Chairman, thank you very much. I appreciate that.

I want to welcome Scott Nichols to the committee today. It's been several years since he's last testified here. I welcome his insights on the NEPA and permitting issues.

Mr. Nichols brings a unique perspective to this in that he is the Permitting Manager for U.S. Geothermal which is headquartered in Boise, Idaho. U.S. Geothermal is an electrical generating company that uses geothermal resources and has a very interesting way of creating electricity.

I want to speak for just a moment on behalf of Senate Bill 279, the Public Lands Renewable Energy Development Act. This bill would allow Federal Government to lease public lands to renewable energy firms. If enacted this bill would return the money collected to the State and county where the project occurs.

Additionally, funding will be provided through that act to the Renewable Energy Resource Conservation Fund which would conserve vital wildlife habitat and enhance public access to Federal lands. I'm very pleased that the majority of the profits incurred will go directly to the State and local governments who can then decide for themselves how best to use those funds.

Additionally the bill is widely supported by over 25 sportsmen's organizations, who represent millions of Americans who enjoy accessing their public lands. Support has also been voiced by such groups as the Western Governors Association, the National Association of Counties, you'll be glad to hear, Commissioner, and the Congressional Sportsmen Foundation, to name a few.

With all the positive feedback we've heard I urge my fellow Senators to support it as well. This is truly a bipartisan effort. I'm happy to work with my colleagues on both sides of the aisle to ensure final passage.

It will go a long ways toward getting these renewable energy resources permitted and on track and do good things for the locals.

Thank you very much, Madame Chairman.

The CHAIR. Thank you, Senator.

Mr. Kidwell, why don't we begin with you?

As we noticed, 5 minutes each and we'll try to keep you to that time. We'll have a few questions afterwards.

Please begin.

STATEMENT OF SCOTT KIDWELL, DIRECTOR OF GOVERN-MENT AND PUBLIC AFFAIRS, COG OPERATING LLC, ON BE-HALF OF CONCHO RESOURCES, INC

Mr. KIDWELL. Thank you, Madame Chair, Ranking Member Murkowski, members of the committee.

Good afternoon, my name is Scott Kidwell. I am the Director of Government Affairs for Concho Resources. I'm here today to express Concho's strong support of S. 2440.

By way of background I would like to tell you a little bit about Concho. We are a publicly traded, independent oil and gas producer, headquartered in Midland, Texas. The entirety of our assets are located in the Permian Basin which is in Southeastern New Mexico and West Texas.

The Permian Basin currently is the largest onshore oil basin in the United States. Currently Concho is the largest producer of oil in the State of New Mexico by a factor of two to the nearest producer.

Concho has significant BLM operations on BLM properties. We operate over 1,000 Federal wells in New Mexico. We have a non operating interest in several hundred other wells located on Federal lands.

Concho estimates that it will invest 8 to $10 billion over the next 5 years in Eddy and Lea Counties, New Mexico which are where the most productive of the Federal lands lie in New Mexico.

Because of the prolific potential that we see in the Permian Basin Concho has announced a 3-year acceleration plan in November 2013 whereby we hope to double our production of oil in the Permian Basin over the next 3 years. As a result you can tell that Concho is vitally concerned with the Federal Government's policy regarding development of energy on Federal lands.

In Concho's experience in New Mexico the APD program, pilot program, has been a success to the extent that we have received more permits than we would have had there not—the program not been in place. Should the program expire in the Carlsbad office alone, who is already down 18 job positions, 41 vacancies would occur that are directly related to APD processing. That would have a catastrophic impact on the pace and volume of processing of APDs.

The BLM field office will soon be asked to implement additional rules regarding hydraulic fracturing. These additional responsibilities will place additional strain on the work force thus making the expiration of the APD program, pilot program, a far worse disaster.

Currently it takes a Concho permit an average of 133 days to be approved. This is in comparison to 2011 when the average APD time was 80 days. The number of filed APDs and the BLM processing time is increasing on a daily basis as additional companies, outside of Concho, turn their focus to drilling and exploring in the Permian Basin.

The stakes at risk here are enormous. Oil and gas is the powerful economic driver and job creator in New Mexico.

Oil and gas is responsible for 30,000 direct jobs in New Mexico.

The 31.5 percent of the general fund for the State of New Mexico is derived from oil and gas activities.

The 96.6 percent of the land grant general fund which funds New Mexico's educational system comes from oil and gas.

Eighty-six percent of the State's severance taxes came from oil and gas production.

In fiscal year 2013, $835 million of Federal royalties were paid for oil and gas production on Federal lands in New Mexico.

Forty-eight percent of which is returned to the State of New Mexico.

We anticipate, as a company, paying $105 million in Federal royalties this year for production in the State of New Mexico.

As you can readily see the investment of a Federal dollar in the permitting program produces many multiples of that investment in return.

With regard to the specifics of this bill, Concho believes the provision of the bill setting a statutory APD fee of $9,500 with the guarantee that 75 percent of the revenues generated would go to the BLM State office where the fee gets collected to be an admirable compromise in bringing more timeliness and predictability to getting the permits you're going to encourage companies to invest in Federal lands.

Concho also supports the provision of the bill that requires the Secretary to consider the factors that the Chairwoman mentioned earlier in her comments. All 4 of those factors are relevant and appropriate. It would bring a focus and an ability to transition to bring folks to offices that are important where the activity is thriving such as in the Permian Basin where we would be able to get proper staffing permit review commensurate with the production potential of the Basin.

Failing to take steps to improve the permit approval times will absolutely ensure drilling starts on Federal lands decline. For a State like New Mexico, that's awfully bad news, particularly as the State is trying to climb out of the most recent recession.

In summary, I would say that S. 2440 is a unique opportunity to increase drilling on Federal lands and increase all the jobs and economic opportunities that come with it. In a nutshell S. 2440 is a common sense jobs and economic opportunity bill. I would urge Congress that it do all it can to facilitate its enactment this year.

On behalf of Concho I want to thank the committee for inviting me today to express our views on S. 2440. I'm happy to answer any questions and happy to provide any other information that might be helpful to the committee.

Thank you.
[The prepared statement of Mr. Kidwell follows:]

PREPARED STATEMENT OF SCOTT M. KIDWELL, DIRECTOR OF GOVERNMENT AND
PUBLIC AFFAIRS, COG OPERATING LLC, ON BEHALF OF CONCHO RESOURCES, INC

My name is Scott M. Kidwell. I am the Director of Government and Public Affairs
for COG Operating LLC, the operating arm of Concho Resources, Inc., ("Concho").
I am here today in strong support of S. 2440, "The BLM Permit Processing Improvement Act of 2014", introduced initially by Senator Tom Udall and Senator John
Barrasso, and co-sponsored by a dozen of their bi-partisan colleagues, five of whom
serve on this Committee. I urge the Committee to do all it can to move Congress
to enact S. 2440 prior to the end of 2014 to avoid the scheduled expiration of the
current authorization of the BLM's pilot program for expediting the processing of
applications for drilling permits (APD).

Concho is a publicly traded independent oil and gas producer headquartered in
Midland, Texas. Concho is engaged in the acquisition, development and exploration
of oil and natural gas properties. Concho's core operating areas are located in the
Permian Basin region of Southeastern New Mexico and West Texas, the largest onshore oil and gas basin in the United States. Currently, Concho is one of the largest
Permian oil and gas operators, producing over 100,000 Boepd in the first quarter
of 2014 and running 33 drilling rigs. Concho is the largest oil producer in New Mexico by a factor of two compared to the next largest producer in that state. Concho
has substantial operations on Bureau of Land Management (BLM) land in New
Mexico, where we have over 257,000 gross acres of BLM land under lease. Illus-
trating the importance of our New Mexico presence, Concho operates over 1,000 federal wells in New Mexico and has a non-operating interest in hundreds of other federal wells. Additionally, Concho has identified many promising undrilled locations
on its BLM acreage and plans to spend between $8 and $10 billion over the next
five years in Eddy and Lea Counties alone, which is where much of the most productive federal energy lands are located. Because of the prolific potential Concho
sees in the Permian Basin, in November 2013 Concho announced a three year acceleration plan to double our production there. As a result, Concho is vitally concerned
with the federal government's policy for energy development on federal lands.

In Concho's view, the bi-partisan effort to reauthorize the BLM's program to improve the review process for APDs presents a welcome alignment of the interests
held by the private sector, the federal government, and state government with regard to developing our national energy resources. All those entities have a common
interest in the expanded supply of the nation's energy resources, the desire to create
private sector jobs in energy development, and the need to generate royalty revenue
to defray governmental expenditures during this challenging budgetary era. Recent
technological advances in US oil and natural gas development have proved to be a
"game changer" for America's energy security and the Nation's economic recovery,
and have provided hundreds of thousands of jobs and billions of dollars in much-
needed federal and state government royalty revenues. As a Nation, we need to
keep expanding that good fortune and not let the opportunity slip away.

At the heart of this favorable development is the ability for domestic oil and gas
producers to secure permits to develop energy properties on private and public
lands. Recent oil and gas development on private lands has far exceeded development on federal lands. As far back as 2005, Congress recognized this critical reality
and took action in Section 365 of the Energy Policy Act to improve oil and gas permitting in seven of the key BLM offices responsible for nearly 70% of the APDs
BLM was handling. Congress's intent in Section 365 was to put more personnel and
financial resources to work in these key offices to accelerate the APD review process
in order to expedite issuance of federal permits to drill.

In Concho's individual experience, that APD pilot program has been enormously
successful and has been responsible for facilitating the issuance of many more APDs
in New Mexico than would have otherwise been the case in the absence of the pilot
program. But all of the benefits for the federal government, the state governments
and the private sector derived from increased oil and gas production attributable to
the pilot program are at risk should the authorization for the pilot program expire.
We understand that should the pilot program expire, the Carlsbad office alone—
which already has 18 vacant positions—stands to lose 41 positions currently authorized for APD review. This would have a catastrophic impact on the pace and volume
of the processing of APDs and would dramatically reduce the production of the federal energy resources and its associated revenue that otherwise could be and would
be developed were APDs to be issued. It is also important to recall that among the
many demands placed on their time the BLM field offices will soon be required to

implement new rules related to hydraulic fracturing, and possibly new requirements on venting and flaring. These additional responsibilities will place additional layers of work and strain on an already shorthanded workforce.

Thus far in 2014, Concho has submitted 86 APDs to the Carlsbad field office and anticipates filing 120 more during the remainder of the year. Currently, it takes a Concho permit an average of 133 days to be approved. By way of comparison, Concho submitted 274 APDs in 2011 with an average approval time of 80 days. The number of filed APDs and the BLM processing time is increasing on a daily basis as additional companies besides Concho sharpen their focus on drilling in the Permian Basin. The Carlsbad office's internal numbers evidence this increase in activity as they report having received 740 APDs through May of FY-14 as compared to 581 APDs for the same time period in FY-13. It is also instructive to note that, except for geologists and engineers, the same BLM staff members who handle APDs are required to review right of way applications for energy development projects and it is estimated that right of way applications in the Carlsbad office have increased by a multiple of ten in calendar year 2014.

Viewed through the perspective of our federal land operations in New Mexico, the stakes at risk are enormous because the oil and gas industry is such a powerful economic engine and job creator in New Mexico. It is estimated that the oil and gas industry creates 30,000 direct jobs in New Mexico, a number which does not reflect the thousands of additional indirect jobs that are generated by the industry. Moreover, 31.5% of New Mexico's general fund revenues are attributable to oil and gas production in the state. As importantly, 96.6% of the Land Grant Permanent Fund- which funds New Mexico's educational system-is derived from oil and gas development and 86% of the state's severance tax revenues come from oil and gas production. In FY-13, $835 million in royalties were paid to the Office of Natural Resource Revenue for oil and gas production on federal land in New Mexico, 48% of which was returned to New Mexico. Concho anticipates paying federal royalties approximating $105 million in 2014, of which 48% will be forwarded to New Mexico. In addition, the local governments in New Mexico rely on oil and gas property tax assessments (ad valorem production taxes and production equipment taxes) which in FY-12 totaled $154 million. The simple fact is that federal, state and local government benefit mightily from increased oil and gas development in New Mexico and the pilot program has been critically important in facilitating oil and gas production and its attendant revenues that accrue to each level of government. The investment of a federal dollar in the permitting program produces many multiples of that investment in return. When these revenue streams are added to the value of the jobs and economic activity created by the oil and gas industry, the public policy case for continuation of the permitting program is compelling.

With regard to the provisions of S. 2440 itself, we observe that it is a balanced piece of legislation that brings appropriate modifications to the management of the APD pilot program at a cost which industry can accept. We are not alone in that assessment given that the bill has drawn the support of a broad spectrum of our industry.

In particular, I would like the Committee to recognize that Concho strongly supports the long term extension of the BLM's Processing Improvement Fund which pays for the permitting program. We find that the provision of the bill setting a statutory APD processing fee of $9,500 indexed annually for inflation, with the guarantee that 75% of the revenues generated would go to the BLM state office where the fee was collected, to be a fair compromise. That trade-off assures producers that they will see a direct benefit from paying the increased fee through having more BLM staff reviewers and a more responsive review process in the local BLM office for their projects. In bringing more timeliness and predictability to getting their permit applications reviewed, the compromise also will provide greater incentive to invest in developments on federal lands.

Concho also supports the provision of the bill that requires the Secretary, in allocating funds raised by the bill among BLM offices, to consider the number of APDs received in an office, the backlog of APDs in an office, the publicly available industry forecast of development of oil and gas under the jurisdiction of an office, and opportunities for partnering with local industry to coordinate and process APDs. All those factors are relevant and appropriate and will, in our opinion, insure that priority federal lands such as the Permian Basin would get proper staffing for permit review commensurate with their production potential.

We believe that with this increased funding from the new statutory APD fee, BLM will be able to compress review times for individual APDs by hiring and retaining sufficient competent personnel to conduct the reviews. It is not in Concho's interest as a key economic engine and employer in the state, nor is it in the interest of the federal government, state or local governments to create backlogs and slow processing times for permits. Failing to take steps to improve permit approval times will absolutely insure a decline in drilling starts on federal lands. Viewed in its local context, this failure would be particularly bad news for New Mexico. New Mexico's economy continues to struggle with a 6.5 percent unemployment rate. Employment figures from June 2014 indicate that for the first time in nine months the state just slightly increased the number of new jobs created compared to the number it lost. But the employment situation remains fragile. It is imperative that federal policy not make things worse.

Ultimately it is the American people who benefit in so many ways from the increased development of the oil and gas resources they already own. Increased domestic production, particularly new production from federal lands which has not kept pace with the recent explosion of production on private land, improves the Nation's energy security, economic welfare, international competitiveness and strategic leverage in world commerce and politics. In S. 2440, we have the opportunity to increase drilling on federal lands and increase all the jobs and economic opportunity that comes with it. From that perspective, S. 2440 is a common sense jobs and economic opportunity bill and Congress ought to do all it can to facilitate its enactment this year.

In conclusion, I strongly urge the Energy Committee to do all it can to move S. 2440 to enactment this year. It is a well-balanced, important and bi-partisan piece of legislation that deserves your attention and effort.

On behalf of Concho, I want to thank the Committee for inviting me today to express our views on S. 2440. I am happy to answer any questions or to provide any further information which might be helpful to the Committee.

The CHAIR. Thank you very much.

Ms. Sgamma.

STATEMENT OF KATHLEEN SGAMMA, VICE PRESIDENT OF GOVERNMENT AND PUBLIC AFFAIRS, WESTERN ENERGY ALLIANCE

Ms. SGAMMA. Thank you, Madame Chair, Ranking Member Murkowski and members of the committee.

I'm Kathleen Sgamma, Vice President of Government Affairs for Western Energy Alliance. We represent about 480 companies engaged in all aspects of environmentally responsible oil and natural gas exploration in the West. We are proud to provide about a quarter of the Nation's natural gas and about 21 percent of its oil production while disturbing less than a tenth of a percent of public lands.

Really appreciate the ability to talk today about S. 2440 today. We have seen, as we've discussed earlier, you know, the dramatic production in oil and natural gas in this country. But it's mostly the result of private sector innovation on private and State lands. The Congressional Resource Service, the Research Service, found that about 96 percent of the increase in oil production since 2007 has been from private lands.

So I think, you know, we were talking about the numbers earlier and it's a little hard, you know. In some places it's up, like New Mexico and Wyoming, where the Federal production is up for oil. But overall in the system it's simply not keeping pace with adjacent private and State lands. I think that's what the CRS found.

So I think that S. 2440 is a partial solution to that problem in that by directing funding to those field offices that have the heaviest APD work flow we will see processing of those permits in a more timely manner, hopefully. We, Western Energy Alliance, particularly supports the bill because there's that direct funding to the originating field office so that unlike the current system where it's

7 named field offices. Funding will naturally flow to those field offices that have the heaviest work flow.

So we appreciate that flexibility in the program that will be an improvement from the current pilot office program.

We really emphasize and appreciate the committee holding this hearing today and taking up this bill. We think it needs to be put in place, as Mr. Kornze noted and other BLM field managers have noted to us and our members, is that without that long term ability to plan and provide assurance to new employees coming on, they're certainly hesitant to hire if they think the funding might run out in 2015. That's why we urge the committee to act on this bill this year and the Senate to act on this bill this year.

Although companies already return $54.12 for every taxpayer dollar BLM spends administering the onshore oil and gas program, our members are willing to agree to the increase in the APD fee and the reduction in the royalty overpayment because of the fact, well for two reasons.

First of all, the funding more naturally flows to the field offices with the heaviest work flow.

Second, it provides regulatory certainty over the next 10 years that that fee won't increase except with the cost of living.

So that's why Western Energy Alliance strongly supports that bill and is willing to, you know, industry is willing to put that extra money on the table.

I would note that since we already pay for inspections, administration, permitting, leasing, environmental analysis, any administration of that onshore program, more than 54 times over. We don't believe new fees should be enacted, but we are, you know, we are willing to support the fees in S. 2440.

So we appreciate the bill and urge the Senate to act on it this year.

Thank you very much for your time today.

[The prepared statement of Ms. Sgamma follows:]

PREPARED STATEMENT OF KATHLEEN SGAMMA, VICE PRESIDENT OF GOVERNMENT AND PUBLIC AFFAIRS, WESTERN ENERGY ALLIANCE

The dramatic growth in domestic oil and natural gas production has been truly transformational. States such as North Dakota and New Mexico are reaping huge economic rewards including significant tax and royalty revenue. North Dakota has experienced large budget surpluses over the last few years and has cut personal taxes because of the oil and natural gas industry. Other states in the West could experience that same type of economic growth if the administration would encourage development in areas where it has the most control—on federal public lands.

The huge increase in U.S. oil and natural gas production over the last several years is the result of private sector investment in technology and improved techniques applied largely on private lands. 96% of the oil production growth since 2007 has been on private and state lands, according to the Congressional Research Service. A recent Energy Information Administration (EIA) report shows that overall fossil fuel production on federal lands is down 7% from the last fiscal year. The report shows a 9% drop in federal onshore natural gas production, with most of the decrease coming from Wyoming where the percentage of federal production is the highest. Oil production on federal lands in the West is up 29% since 2008, but that significantly lags the 93% increase on adjacent private and state lands.

S. 2440 the BLM Permit Processing Improvement Act of 2014 is a partial solution to reversing that trend. I would like to thank Chairman Landrieu for holding this hearing today, and Senator Tom Udall for the bill along with co-sponsoring Senators Barrasso, Bennet, Enzi, Hatch, Heinrich, Heitkamp, Heller, Hoeven, Inhofe, Lee, Tester, Udall and Walsh. The level of bipartisan support is truly encouraging.

By ensuring a portion of the Application for Permit to Drill (APD) fee paid by oil and natural gas companies goes directly to APD processing at the originating field office, the bill will provide much-needed resources to the Bureau of Land Management (BLM). By directing that funding to APD processing, the bill will ensure BLM has the resources to support revenue-generating oil and natural gas development, while strengthening western economies and the nation's energy security.

Action is required on S. 2440 this year because the Pilot Office program for permitting, created by the Energy Policy Act of 2005, expires at the end of the 2015 fiscal year. The ten-year reauthorization provides an opportunity to inject some much needed flexibility into the program. The seven pilot offices designated in EPAct may have been busy in 2005, but ten years later market conditions have changed dramatically. Some pilot offices have seen activity fall off while other field offices that were relatively sleepy in 2005 have experienced huge increases in workload.

If the program is allowed to lapse without a replacement, BLM will experience a significant reduction in the resources necessary to process APDs, and we would experience even longer processing times and less production on federal lands. The EPAct 2005 Pilot Office program, which directs rental fees to the seven named Pilot Offices, provided permit funding in a limited way. S. 2440 aims to replace that funding while providing more flexibility to ensure funds are spent at the field offices with the heaviest APD workflow, not just a static list of seven.

Western Energy Alliance supports the bill's $3,000 increase in the APD fee, from the current $6,500, and the reduction in the interest rate for royalty overpayments to direct those funds to APD processing. Even though producers already return $54.12 for every taxpayer dollar BLM spends administering the entire onshore program, we are willing to agree to those two cost increases because the bill provides regulatory certainty that rulemaking to increase APD fees will not take place for the next ten years. In addition, targeting the funds more directly to BLM field offices according to APD workflow is important to Alliance members.

Western Energy Alliance urges the Committee to act this year on S.2440. We hear reports from busy BLM field offices that they are already starting to feel the pinch of the impending September 2015 deadline. Field managers cannot hire replacements to handle APD workloads when positions become available because they do not know whether the funding for those hires will continue beyond 2015. Rural communities across the West, such as Farmington, New Mexico, Vernal, Utah and Pinedale, Wyoming depend on oil and natural gas development on federal lands for a significant portion of their economic prosperity. Passage of S. 2440 will help ensure job creation in western communities.

About Western Energy Alliance

Western Energy Alliance represents over 480 companies engaged in all aspects of environmentally responsible exploration and production of oil and natural gas across the West. The Alliance represents independents, the majority of which are small businesses with an average of fifteen employees. Because of the predominance of public lands in the West, our members regularly operate on public lands to provide to the American people the energy owned by all. Our members are proud to provide 25% of America's natural gas and 21% of its oil production while disturbing only 0.07% of public lands.

The CHAIR. Thank you.
Commissioner Christensen.

STATEMENT OF MARK A. CHRISTENSEN, CHAIRMAN, CAMPBELL COUNTY BOARD OF COMMISSIONERS, ON BEHALF OF THE WYOMING COUNTY COMMISSIONERS ASSOCIATION

Mr. CHRISTENSEN. Good afternoon, Madame Chair, Ranking Member Murkowski, Senator Barrasso and the distinguished members of the committee. Thank you for the opportunity to address you today regarding opportunities to more efficiently process permits for energy production on Federal lands.

My name is Mark Christensen and I'm the Chairman of the Board of Campbell County Commissioners in Wyoming. I'm also here on behalf of the Wyoming County Commissioners Association, representing all 23 Wyoming counties.

Campbell County produces approximately 10.6 quadrillion BTUs of energy annually providing from one county about 10 percent of the entire country's energy demand. Many of you know we produce approximately 40 percent of the Nation's coal. What you may not know is that Campbell County is also the top producer of crude oil in Wyoming.

Almost all of this coal and oil is produced on Federal lands. To produce energy to fuel America at this volume we are heavily dependent on the efficiency and effectiveness of our local BLM field office in Buffalo, Wyoming. This is why we are grateful to Senators Udall and Barrasso as well as the bipartisan co-sponsors of S. 2440, the BLM Permit Processing Improvement Act of 2014.

The bill before you today was born from a pilot project which is particularly important to Campbell County as the BLM Buffalo field office was one of 7 pilot project offices designated by Congress in the Energy Policy Act of 2005 or EPACT 2005.

At the start of the 21st century Wyoming and specifically Campbell County experienced a dramatic boom in coal bed methane or CBM drilling. Applications for permits to drill or APDs began to quickly stack up in the Buffalo field office. With a staff at the time of less than 30 people the BLM's Buffalo field office was simply unprepared to handle the volume of work.

By 2003 the Buffalo field office had a backlog of around 3,000 APDs with no end in sight.

Campbell County along with our neighbor counties and private sector stakeholders sought relief from Congress through our Federal delegation and Congress delivered by creating the pilot project program in EPACT 2005. As a result the Buffalo field office was able to more than triple their staff and add about 25 additional people who were dedicated to oil and gas operations.

The legislation before you today would remove the pilot from the pilot program and make necessary changes to allow for greater funds in offices with high permitting demands. The bill includes important flexibility for the Secretary of the Interior and State offices to redirect funds to new offices as demand dictates. Directing resources back to States and field offices that will generate significant revenue for the Federal Government is sound fiscal policy and also sound energy and environmental policy.

In 2013 oil and gas production in Wyoming generated over $400 million in royalty revenue for the Federal Government. When you add in the rest of Wyoming's minerals, the total revenue collected and kept by the Federal Government was well in excess of $1 billion.

S. 2440 would specifically direct the permit fees back to the States where those fees are collected. These fees will result in more timely issued APDs and therefore, greater Federal royalties.

A critical component to the timely processing and approval of APDs is site visits. In Wyoming these site visits often require driving for several hours. These visits to multiple sites are long and remove the BLM employee from the office for days at a time resulting in time not spent doing the necessary analysis and work to ensure that permits are completed accurately.

As permits are filed by the hundreds or even thousands, the permit backlog can quickly become unmanageable. Added staff capacity made possible by the bill means more teams covering site visits allowing for a much more efficient process.

While 2003 was frustrating what we didn't face then was the dramatic pressure of private lands oil and gas development in places like North Dakota and Texas.

Today operators know that if they cannot get a timely permit in Wyoming they have somewhere else to go. This is already happening with oil and gas production on Federal lands decreasing again last year as capital fled to private land plays. That is bad news for Federal coffers and terrible news for local economies and heavy public land States and counties.

It is important to realize that the bill is also sound energy and environmental policy. Offices like the Buffalo field office have a great many responsibilities to manage public lands for multiple uses, including recreation and wildlife conservation. When an office is overwhelmed by sudden and dramatic increases in oil and gas related work all of their programs suffer.

The increased production generated from the timely issuance of APDs by BLM benefits not just the State of Wyoming and its counties, but the entire U.S. because of the large Federal land and mineral ownership in Wyoming and shifts the reliance for energy from foreign sources to domestic.

We strongly support speedy passage of S. 2440 for all the reasons already mentioned. We are particularly pleased by the oil and gas industry's willingness to increase permit fees in order to make this reauthorization possible. This is an example of all parties coming together to improve a process that benefits the U.S. Treasury, States, counties and industry.

However, I'd be remiss if I didn't mention that producing quality environmental impact documents and accurate and timely permits cannot depend entirely on industry dollars alone. Local governments, State governments, private sector interest groups and Federal agencies all must play a role.

Madame Chair, thank you for the opportunity today. I am happy to answer any questions you may have.

[The prepared statement of Mr. Christensen follows:]

PREPARED STATEMENT OF MARK A. CHRISTENSEN, CHAIRMAN, CAMPBELL COUNTY BOARD OF COMMISSIONERS, ON BEHALF OF THE WYOMING COUNTY COMMISSIONERS ASSOCIATION

Good afternoon Madam Chair, Ranking Member Murkowski, Senator Barrasso, and distinguished members of the committee. Thank you for the opportunity to address you today regarding opportunities to more efficiently process permits for energy production on federal lands.

My name is Mark Christensen, I am the Chairman of the Board of County Commissioners in Campbell County, Wyoming, located in northeastern Wyoming. I am also here on behalf of the Wyoming County Commissioners Association representing all 23 Wyoming counties. Campbell County produces approximately 10.6 quadrillion BTU's of energy annually, providing from one county about 10% of the entire country's energy demand.

While a great many of those BTU's come from the enormous deposits of low sulfur coal in the Powder River Basin, Campbell County is also the top producer of crude oil in Wyoming. Almost all of this is produced on federal lands. To produce energy to fuel America at this volume, we are heavily dependent on the efficiency and effectiveness of our local BLM field office in Buffalo, Wyoming. That is why we are grateful to Senators Udall and Barrasso, as well as the bi-partisan co-sponsors of S.2440, the BLM Permit Processing Improvement Act of 2014.

History of the Pilot Project Program in Campbell County

The pilot project program is particularly important to us in Campbell County because the BLM Buffalo field office was one of seven pilot project offices designated by Congress in the Energy Policy Act of 2005 (EPAct 05). During the earliest years of the 21st century, Wyoming in general, but Campbell County in particular, experienced a dramatic boom in Coal Bed Methane, or CBM, drilling. CBM is a natural gas extracted from coal seams not yet mined. It is a process that produces high quality, pipeline-ready gas that requires little processing before sale.

Applications for permits to drill (APDs) began to quickly stack up in the Buffalo field office. With a staff at the time of less than 30 people, the BLM's Buffalo field office was simply unprepared to handle the volume of work about to fall on them. By 2003, the Buffalo field office had a backlog of around 3,000 APDs with no end in sight.

Campbell County, along with our neighbor counties and private sector stakeholders, actively sought relief from Congress through our federal delegation; and at least for us, our delegation and Congress truly delivered by creating the pilot project program in EPAct 05. As a result, the Buffalo field office was able to more than triple their staff, and add about 25 additional people dedicated to oil and gas operations.

Ten years later, I am here today because our on-the-ground experience with the pilot project leads us to believe that it should no longer be a pilot program, and should no longer be limited to 7 offices. As a county association, we join our state partners at the Western Governors' Association in support of S.2440.

BLM Permit Processing Improvement Act of 2014

The legislation before you today would remove the "pilot" from the pilot program, and make necessary changes to allow for greater funds in offices with high permitting demands. Additionally, the legislation gives greater flexibility to the BLM to direct these funds to new areas as production demands shift. I want to take a moment to discuss both of these important changes as it relates to my county and state.

First, directing resources back to states and field offices that will generate significant revenue for the federal government is sound fiscal policy, and also sound energy and environmental policy.

In 2013, oil and gas production in Wyoming generated over $400 million dollars in royalty revenue for the federal government. When you add in the rest of Wyoming's minerals, the total revenue collected and kept by the federal government was well in excess of $1 billion dollars. Yet, the BLM's state office in Wyoming had a total 2013 budget of only $115 million dollars for all their programs statewide. S.2440 would help correct that imbalance by specifically directing permit fees to return to the states where those fees are collected, providing a major return on investment to the U.S. Treasury.

It isn't simply a matter of the dollar for dollar imbalance of what Wyoming generates and what BLM's Wyoming state office receives, rather; directing APD fees back to a state with high APD demand will help generate more timely permits. More timely permits will result in even greater federal royalties to the U.S. Treasury in a time when non-tax revenue is highly coveted. A concrete example of how the bill would result in faster permit times is simply to understand the work flow of a single APD filed in the Buffalo field office, where the length of time to issue an APD from Notice of Survey is approximately 300 days and the time once all information is received is approximately 9 days. This is a major improvement from pre-pilot project days, though we believe additional improvement may still be possible.

A critical component to the timely processing and approval of APDs is site visits. In Wyoming, often these site visits require driving for several hours, often on gravel roads. When grouped together as they often are, these visits are long and remove the BLM employee from the office for days at a time. Those are days not spent doing the necessary analysis and work to ensure that permits are completed accurately. As permits are filed by the hundreds or even thousands, the permit backlog becomes unbearable as it did back in 2003. Added staff capacity made possible by the bill before you today means more teams covering site visits, allowing for a much more efficient process.

While 2003 was frustrating, what we didn't face then was the dramatic pressure of private lands oil and gas development in places like North Dakota and Texas. Today, operators know that if they cannot get a timely permit in Wyoming, they have somewhere else to go. In fact, all the data on oil and gas production in the United States indicates that is already happening. Oil and gas production on federal lands decreased again last year as capital fled to these private lands plays. That is bad news for federal coffers and terrible news for local economies in heavy public lands states and counties.

The energy companies within our state and county compete for capital with divisions across the U.S. Delays in the timely permitting of APDs makes states with federal lands, and the federal lands and/or mineral estates, less attractive for development. In a state and county which rely on severance taxes and ad-valorem taxes from the extraction of minerals, timely approvals of APDs is critical to the long-term health and prosperity of our citizens and our communities.

It is important to realize that the bill before you today is also sound energy and environment policy. BLM offices like the Buffalo field office have a great many responsibilities to manage public lands for multiple uses, including recreation and wildlife conservation. When an office is completely overwhelmed by sudden and dramatic increases in oil and gas related work, all of their programs are impacted even if they are not directly related to oil and gas operations. This should be a concern to those interested in rangeland monitoring, sage grouse conservation activities, maintaining recreational activities, and the many other tasks of the BLM.

The final important component of S.2440 that I want to briefly mention is the flexibility granted to the Secretary of the Interior and to state offices to redirect funds to new offices as demand dictates. Again, Wyoming has a unique perspective on this.

Thanks to the leadership of U.S. Representative Cynthia Lummis, last year the pilot project dollars directed toward the Buffalo field office were redirected one rung up on the administrative ladder to the BLM's High Plains district office in Casper, Wyoming. This minor adjustment allowed BLM to shift resources from Buffalo to Casper to help meet the new demands coming from Converse County, my neighbor to the south. The Casper field office expects about 5,000 APDs to come their way from new oil and gas development in Converse County. It only makes sense to allow the flexibility of meeting new demands when they arise.

The rates of growth we are talking about are significant. Year-over-year oil production increase for Campbell County and Converse County between calendar year 2012 and calendar year 2013 was 33% and 49% respectively. A comparison for the first five months of 2014 indicates a production increase of 30% when compared to the 2013 production for Campbell County, with an additional 25% production increase for Converse County. This increased production benefits not just the State of Wyoming and its counties, but the entire U.S. because of the large federal land and mineral ownership in Wyoming, and shifts the reliance for energy from foreign sources to domestic.

Industry Money isn't Everything

We strongly support speedy passage of S.2440 for all the reasons already mentioned. We are particularly pleased by the oil and gas industry's willingness to increase permit fees in order to make this reauthorization possible. To us this is just another example of how the oil and gas industry of today is making great strides at being good neighbors in the communities they operate in.

However, because the theme of this hearing is on examining ways to break the logjam of permits on federal lands, I would be remiss if I didn't mention that producing quality environmental impact documents and accurate and timely permits cannot entirely depend on industry dollars alone. Local governments, state governments, private sector interest groups and federal agencies all must play a constructive role.

For us in Wyoming, we take that role seriously and engage with our federal partners at every possible opportunity. For those of us in a position to do so, we also have been willing to spend money from our own coffers to improve and bolster data on sensitive or protected species. Today, Campbell County is exploring ways to help the BLM gather comprehensive, region-wide data on raptors so that all of us are on the same page when it comes to where these birds are, and how activity affects their behavior. We have already completed an initial study identifying nests within Campbell County and Johnson County, and are working now to expand upon this project through a partnership with the Buffalo field office which would bring Campbell County monies into the effort. These kinds of partnerships are occurring all over Wyoming with industry, local governments, and environmental stewardship groups.

If we want to take another large step toward reducing bottlenecks, it is exactly this kind of cooperative approach that should be encouraged and incentivized. By necessity, this will mean actively seeking to discourage and remove incentives for litigation. Decisions on land use in the West will almost always cause tension. However, that tension need not cause conflict, and litigation is by its very nature, conflict. Groups that spend all their time and effort in the courtroom are a major contributor to the overall backlog. Rather than trying to affect policy behind the closed doors of a courtroom, we are all better served by doing the difficult work of finding consensus and putting boots-on-the-ground toward actual environmental stewardship.

I add that Wyoming is at the forefront with regard to laws and regulations which deal with environmental impact, and we take the environment within our state very seriously. Ranchers may have been Wyoming's original land stewards, but today, the energy industry is a major part of this process. Protection of Wyoming's environment also makes good financial sense. Though Wyoming's number one economic generator is mineral extraction, tourism is number two.

Madam Chair, thank you again for the opportunity today. I am happy to answer any questions you may have.

The CHAIR. Thank you, Commissioner. I am looking forward to visiting Campbell County. I'm very interested in what you all are doing there. So as soon as I can get there, I will.

Thank you.

Mr. CHRISTENSEN. We would invite you.

The CHAIR. Commissioner Wichman.

STATEMENT OF COMMISSIONER LORINDA WICHMAN, NYE COUNTY COMMISSION, PRESIDENT-ELECT, NEVADA ASSOCIATION OF COUNTIES

Ms. WICHMAN. Yes, ma'am. Thank you.

Thank you very much. I would like to thank Chairman Landrieu and the rest of this committee for this incredible opportunity to be here with you in our State capitol and to share a little bit with you from Nevada's outback, or actually the entire country's outback.

I'd also like to take a moment to thank Senator Heller and his staff for making this possible for me to do this.

In addition, a personal thank you to you for addressing the WIR in New Orleans. Everybody was extremely pleased with that.

My name is Lorinda Wichman.

I'm Commissioner from Nye County's District One.

I'm Vice Chair of our Commission.

I'm also the Chairman for the Nye, White Pine, Eureka and Lander County's Secure Rural Schools Resource Advisory Council.

I'm the President Elect for the Nevada's Association of Counties, the Chairman of the Association's Committee on Public Lands and Natural Resources.

I'm an appointee to the State Land Use Planning Advisory Board and Nevada's Representative on the Public Lands Steering Committee of the National Association of Counties.

S. 279 and S. 2440 provide for a more equitable and efficient path to the development of our Nation's diversified energy portfolio. I was once told that a measure of a good legislation was when everyone in the room that left was angered by the legislation and this probably the first opportunity I have seen for the extremely diverse support that this legislation has.

My testimony is in support of the bill on behalf of my neighbors, my Commission District, Nye County and Nevada's Association of Counties and the National Association of Counties. District One of Nye County which is possibly the largest Commissioner's District in the lower 48 States is 17,933 square miles. The county itself is a little over 18,000 square miles.

Included within the boundaries of my district alone are the Nevada National Security site, portions of Nellis Air Force Base, that includes the Nevada test and training range, Ash Meadows National Wildlife Refuge, portions of Death Valley National Park, Yucca Mountain, the Yomba and Duckwater Indian Reservations, Round Mountain Gold, Railroad Valley oil field and the Crescent Dunes Renewable Energy project.

I'm extremely proud to represent that district.

My neighbors in Nye County are proud to host so many recognizable landmarks that provide for our Nation's security. 98 percent of Nye County is owned, managed or controlled by Federal agencies. Ten communities and two reservations spread out over this 18,000 square mile area have forced us to maintain two separate centers of government that are over 150 miles apart.

For perspective once a month I travel 86 miles one way to attend the Commissioner's meeting in the county seat. Once a month I travel 252 miles one way to attend the second Commission meeting which is held in the population center. Gives you an idea of size.

Our operating revenues have steadily declined since 2008, mostly due to the assessed evaluation of the properties which is now one-third of what it was prior to 2008. The county's operating budget for fiscal year 2014–2015 is now only 30 million.

We've reduced our work force by 15 percent. Unfortunately a large part of that reduction was in law enforcement.

We have consolidated services. We've restricted the purchase of non essential supplies. Our infrastructure buildings and grounds are all suffering from lack of improvements or maintenance.

Payments in lieu of taxes provide us with about 2 to $3.5 million a year. That's 33 cents an acre.

Our private, well, that is 10 percent of our budget, as you can tell from the figures. We rely heavily on the PILT program along with 2,000 other counties in this country. PILT is the only program that offsets the losses of our property taxes.

S. 275 needs to be supplemental to that PILT program. It's extremely important to all of us.

Our private property taxes are collected on only 2 percent of Nye County because of the overwhelming Federal presence. Despite the obstacles, Nevada's counties are required to provide essential services to all of the residents and their visitors. Therefore, it's easy to understand why Nye County, the State, the national association, Nevada's Association and all the industries are all in favor of this legislation.

Nevada has an abundance of natural resources. The current management practices and permitting processes to reach our resources have discouraged many from pursuing projects on federally managed lands. The hearty industries that have persevered are building into their feasibility study as much as 8 years and hundreds of thousands of dollars just to get through the process.

The Nevada Associations of County Policy for Renewable Energy Development highlights the role of county officials working with the other agencies to permit appropriate projects on federally managed lands. The policies also promote the use of cooperating agency agreements to assist in the development of resource management plans throughout the State. Without a direct benefit to the host counties there isn't much incentive to spend the time or the taxpayer's money to promote anybody's policy.

Nevada has abundant wind, solar, geothermal, mineral and land resources which position us to be one of the top States in attracting development of alternative energy projects. Streamlining the process to realize the benefits of production is paramount to our future success and allows counties to play a greater role in helping our State recover from the economic crisis.

The CHAIR. I have to ask you to wrap up, if you could.

Ms. WICHMAN. The passage of the legislation will lay the foundation to help industries to generate the funds needed, like counties, to provide critical services to my neighbors, Nye County, Nevada and this Nation.

Thank you.

[The prepared statement of Ms. Wichman follows:]

PREPARED STATEMENT OF COMMISSIONER LORINDA WICHMAN, VICE CHAIRMAN, NYE COUNTY COMMISSION, NV, ON S. 279 AND S. 2440

Good afternoon, I would like to thank Chairman Landrieu and the Committee for this incredible opportunity to share a little with you from the outback of Nevada. I would also like to thank Senator Heller and his staff for making this opportunity possible.

I am Lorinda Wichman, Commissioner of District 1 in Nye County, Nevada and Vice-Chair of the Board. I am also the Chairman of the Nye, White Pine, Eureka and Lander Counties SRS RAC. The President Elect of the Nevada State Association, Chairman of the Association's committee on Public Lands and Natural Resources. I am also a Governor's appointee to the State Land Use Planning Advisory Council and Nevada's representative on the Public Lands Steering Committee of the National Association of Counties.

S.279 and S.2440 provide for a more equitable and efficient path to the development of our nation's diversified energy portfolio. I was once told that the measure of good legislation was when everyone was angered but this legislation has an extremely diverse base of support. My testimony in support of this bill is on behalf of my neighbors, my Commission District, Nye County, the Nevada Association of Counties and the National Association of Counties.

District One of Nye County, which is possibly the largest County Commission District in the lower 48 states, is 17,933 sq. miles. The county itself is 18,210 square miles. Included within the boundaries of my commission district are the Nevada National Security Site, portions of Nellis Air Force Base that include the Nevada Test and Training Range, Ash Meadows National Wildlife Refuge, portions of the Death Valley National Park, Yucca Mountain, the Yomba and Duckwater Indian Reservations, Round Mountain Gold mine, Railroad Valley oil field and the Crescent Dunes renewable energy project.

I am extremely proud to represent this district. My neighbors and Nye County are proud to host so many recognizable landmarks that provide for our nation's security. Ninety-eight percent of Nye County is owned, managed or controlled by the federal government. Ten communities and two reservations spread out over this 18,210 square mile area have forced us to maintain two separate centers of government more than 150 miles apart. For perspective; once a month I travel 86 miles, one way, to attend a commission meeting in the County seat and once a month I travel 252 miles, one way, to attend the second commission meeting held in the population center.

Our operating revenues have steadily declined since 2008 due mostly to the assessed values of property which is one third of the pre 2008 values. The County operating budget for fiscal year 2014/2015 is now only $30 million. We have reduced our workforce by 15% and unfortunately a large part of the reduction was in law enforcement. We have consolidated services and restricted the purchase of non-essential supplies. Our infrastructure, buildings and grounds are suffering from lack of improvements. Payments in lieu of taxes provide us with $2 to $3.5 mil a year, or $.33 per acre. Our private property taxes are collected on only 2% of Nye County because of the overwhelming federal presence. Despite these obstacles Nevada Counties are required to provide essential services to all of their residents and visitors. Therefore, it is easy to understand why Nye County and the state and national associations are encouraging the revenue sharing.

Nevada has an abundance of natural resources. The current management practices and permitting processes to reach our resources have discouraged many from pursuing projects on federally managed lands. The hardy industries that have persevered are building into their feasibility studies as much as eight years and hundreds of thousands of dollars just to get through those processes.

The Nevada Association of Counties policy on renewable energy development highlights the role of County Officials working with other agencies to permit appropriate projects on federally managed lands. The policy also promotes the use of cooperating agency agreements to assist in the development of resource management plans throughout the state. Without a direct benefit to the host counties there isn't much incentive to spend time and taxpayers' money to promote any policy.

Nevada has abundant wind, solar, geothermal, mineral and land resources which position us to be one of the top states in attracting development of alternative energy projects. Streamlining the process to realize the benefits of production is paramount to our future success and allows Counties to play a greater role in helping the state recover from its economic crisis.

Passage of this legislation will lay the foundation to help industry to generate the funds needed by Counties to provide critical services to my neighbors, Nye County, the State of Nevada and our Nation.

The CHAIR. Thank you very much for that beautiful testimony. Please continue.

STATEMENT OF ARTHUR HAUBENSTOCK, CHAIR OF THE UTILITY-SCALE SOLAR POWER DIVISION, SOLAR ENERGY INDUSTRIES ASSOCIATION AND SENIOR COUNSEL, PERKINS COIE LLP

Mr. HAUBENSTOCK. Good afternoon and thank you, Chair Landrieu, Ranking Member Murkowski and members of this committee for your leadership, your support of solar energy and this opportunity to provide testimony on behalf of the Solar Energy Industries Association, known at SEIA.

My name is Arthur Haubenstock. I'm Chair of the Utility-Scale Power Division of SEIA. We're grateful that the committee recognizes the increasingly important contributions solar is making to our Nation's energy supply and the role that our public lands play in achieving the promise of solar energy for the benefit of the Nation.

SEIA represents the entire solar industry including 1,000 member companies and nearly 143,000 American citizens that the industry employs. Solar power transforms the endless, free energy provided by the sun into electric power that drives commerce, industry and our way of life. It is doing so at decreasing cost, without air, water or other emissions and with minimal environmental impact overall.

Solar is a young industry, but it's growing fast. Solar capacity in the United States is now the equivalent of approximately 6 nuclear power plants, enough to power 3 million homes. In the first quarter of this year alone, solar comprised 74 percent of all new electric capacity in the United States. Of that number 75 percent came from utility-scale solar power plants both photovoltaic, known as PV plants and concentrating solar power CSP. This phenomenal growth is the result of private investment, technological innovation, a maturing industry and smart Federal and State policies including the Investment Tax Credit.

Since the inception of the Investment Tax Credit there's been 3,000 percent growth in solar. That's about a compound of growth rate of 77 percent annually. That has been a tremendous investment for the Federal Government. It has received a very strong return and great results. We wanted to thank Senator Heller for his co-sponsorship of the bill to enable the Investment Tax Credit to continue its benefits.

The Investment Tax Credit is currently planned to expire in 2016. That's already creating a chilling effect on investment in the solar industry because of the advanced time needed for financers who are concerned about its expiration. The change in the trigger to commence construction which is what applies to other renewable energy technologies would be tremendously beneficial to ensure that solar continues its tremendous growth and continues to serve the country.

Solar is an energy source that's available in every U.S. Congressional District. It has a supply chain that stretches from coast to coast. Its potential to serve the Nation is far greater than what it's accomplished to date and there's every reason for the United States to be the world leader in solar.

Right now it's not. Germany is actually the solar leader in the world. The solar resource in Germany is equivalent to that of the great State of Alaska. That is very interesting in that June, just this last month, half of the electric supply for Germany came from solar power.

That says two things.

One is that Alaska has great potential to be a solar leader in the world.

Also that the United States isn't quite living up to its potential yet.

There's much that can be done to make sure that that happens.

The opportunities for utility-scale solar are really tremendous across the Southwest, in particular. Much of the best solar resources in the world are located in the Southwest both because of the quality of the sunlight and the proximity to cities and to industrial centers throughout the Southwest. But currently right now only 23 percent of the operating solar capacity of utility-scale is on public lands even though so much of the best resources are on public lands.

But right now there's about a gigawatt of solar power plants under construction on public lands. Only 36 percent of all utility-scale megawatts under construction are on public lands.

We are grateful for the work of the Department of the Interior and the BLM for its implementation of the solar energy program which we are continuing to work with them in their leadership. We want to thank Neil Kornze, Ray Brady and many others for their extensive work to try to improve the opportunities for solar on public lands.

The most important step that could be taken to ensure that the promised incentives of the solar energy program which have not yet materialized are two things.

One is to continue work on the SMART and the STAR program that the Administration has undertaken.

But also to go back to some of the aspects of the fast track permitting processes that were in place in 2010.

In particular the need to establish clear deadlines to have milestone schedules, corrective action when schedules are not met and the opportunity to have corrective action and true accountability at the highest level of agencies enables Federal and State agencies to work very closely together and achieve tremendous permitting processes and timelines. We've seen great results. Those results are starting to slip. But we need to make sure that we can continue that progress.

I want to thank you again for this opportunity to testify and look forward to your questions.

[The prepared statement of Mr. Haubenstock follows:]

PREPARED STATEMENT OF ARTHUR HAUBENSTOCK, CHAIR OF THE UTILITY-SCALE SOLAR POWER DIVISION, SOLAR ENERGY INDUSTRIES ASSOCIATION AND SENIOR COUNSEL, PERKINS COIE LLP

Madam Chairwoman, Ranking Member Murkowski, and Members of the Committee,

Thank you for the opportunity to provide testimony on potential improvements to solar energy development on public lands. I am Arthur Haubenstock, and I serve as Chair of the Utility-Scale Solar Power Division of the Solar Energy Industries Association (SEIA). I am also a Senior Counsel with Perkins Coie, LLP, and my clients include companies developing solar projects on both federal and private lands. I am testifying on behalf of SEIA's 1,000 member companies and the nearly 143,000 American citizens employed by the solar industry. SEIA represents the entire solar industry, encompassing all major solar technologies (photovoltaics, concentrating solar power and solar water heating[1]) and all points in the value chain, including financiers, project developers, component manufacturers and solar installers. Before I begin my testimony, let me thank Chairwoman Landrieu and Ranking Member Murkowski for their leadership and support of solar energy. We are grateful that the Committee recognizes the increasingly important contributions to our energy supply, as well as the role that our public lands play in achieving the promise of solar energy for the benefit of the nation.

I. Introduction

The Solar Energy Industries Association is celebrating its 40th year as the national trade association of the U.S. solar energy industry, having been established in 1974. Through advocacy and education, SEIA and its 1,000 member companies are building a strong solar industry to power America. As the voice of the industry, SEIA works to make solar a mainstream, significant energy source by expanding markets, removing market barriers, strengthening the industry and educating the public on the benefits of solar energy.

Our nation is graced with some of the world's best solar resources, in both the quality and quantity of the sunlight we receive as well as the proximity of our best solar areas to some of the country's largest cities and industries. While excellent opportunities for solar deployment exist throughout the country, much of the best solar resources are in the Southwest, and on public lands.

Our exceptionally rich solar resources have much to offer the nation, its economy and its environment. Solar can contribute substantially to a clean, sustainable domestic energy supply to power growth and prosperity for many decades to come. Its prospects for doing so depend greatly on whether we properly foster this still young, but rapidly maturing, industry. Stable, long-term policies, including tax policies as well as improved permitting processes and access to the nation's best solar resources, are the keystones to realizing solar's promise for the nation.

S. 279, the Public Land Renewable Energy Development Act of 2013, currently before the Senate, demonstrates the remarkable, bipartisan recognition of the tremendous value that solar offers the nation and the commitment to make its benefits available to all Americans. This bill reflects the need to craft policies today that will provide for a clean energy future for tomorrow, one in which our energy comes from renewable, domestic sources. While we have some concerns with the details of this legislation, SEIA looks forward to working with the sponsors to address our concerns. We are pleased to have this opportunity to address them and other factors needed to maintain the U.S. as a worldwide solar leader.

II. The U.S. Solar Industry: Recent Highlights & Future Prospects

In recent years, America's solar industry has come a long way in converting its solar resources to the electrical energy our economy needs to thrive. Solar energy is a young industry, but it is growing fast. In the first quarter of this year, solar

---

[1] For more information on each of these solar technologies, please see SEIA, "Solar Technology," available at http://www.seia.org/policy/solar-technology.

comprised 74% of all of the new electric capacity in the U.S.[2] The vast majority of this new capacity, over 75%, came from utility-scale solar power plants, both photovoltaic (PV) and concentrating solar power (CSP), which collectively added approximately 1,260 MWac to the energy supply.[3] Solar capacity in the U.S. now exceeds 12,820 MWac,[4] the equivalent of approximately six nuclear power plants,[5] and enough to power 3 million homes.[6] The following graph* illustrates solar's remarkable growth since 2000, including anticipated installations this year:

This phenomenal growth is the result of private investment, technological innovation, a maturing industry and smart federal and state policies. The federal government has received a strong return on its investment of public dollars, with benefits to our economy that far exceed their costs.

Solar is an energy source available in every U.S. Congressional district. Although Germany's solar resource is the equivalent of Alaska's, which has comparatively less solar potential than most other States, Germany continues to lead the world in solar installations-with a cumulative 35.7 GWp installed through 2013.[7] In June 2014, for the first time, solar production met over half of Germany's peak demand.[8] The United States, with its far better solar resources, could easily become the world leader in solar energy production.

Although solar is growing quickly, the nation has just begun to tap into its solar resources. Solar's potential to serve the nation is far greater than its remarkable success to date. Solar power transforms the endless, free energy we receive from the sun into electric power to drive commerce, industry and our way of life, at decreasing costs; without air, water or any other emissions; and with minimal environmental impact overall. Solar power plants can provide the nation with enough domestic, fully secure energy to meet the entire country's peak needs, using only a fraction of the solar resources available to us. The recently-released annual forecast published by the U.S. Energy Information Administration (U.S. EIA) projects that through 2040, nearly 40 GW of solar capacity will be installed in this country—approximately three times the currently installed solar capacity, and nearly half of the renewable energy expected to be deployed over the same timeframe.[9] The Bureau of Land Management (BLM) reports that designated Solar Energy Zones on federal lands alone could provide nearly 24 GW of this domestic, clean power;[10] federal lands potentially available for new zones or individual projects could provide much more. Our nation can—and should—depend on its exceptional solar resources to power its exceptional future.

As solar provides increasing amounts of energy to the country, its costs are decreasing dramatically. As shown in the charts below, PV system prices are generally decreasing in every market segment, year-over-year.[11] Solar deployment is paying great dividends to the American economy and continues to act as catalyst to drive down future costs.

The solar industry relies on an increasing labor force and a host of other domestic industries throughout the country, all of which are sharing in solar's success. With increased solar deployment, both the number of direct and indirect jobs, and companies in solar's supply chain, have grown as well. For example, the supply chain for

---

[2] SEIA, "Solar Energy Facts: Q1 2014" (June 16, 2014), a copy of which is included as Attachment 3.

[3] Id.; note that an average 85% conversion factor from DC to AC ratings was applied to reported PV statistics (using 2013 estimates from the National Renewable Energy Laboratory (NREL); see Ong et al, "Land-Use Requirements for Solar Power Plants in the United States" at p. 5 (June 2013)(hereinafter "NREL Land Use Requirements"), available at http://www.nrel.gov/docs/fy13osti/56290.pdf).

[4] Id. (see fn.3 re: conversion factor for PV).

[5] The Duane Arnold Energy Center, for example, has a capacity of 1,912 MW; see U.S. Nuclear Regulatory Commission, "Duane Arnold Energy Center," available at http://www.nrc.gov/info-finder/reactor/duan.html .

[6] SEIA, "Solar Energy Facts: Q1 2014."

* Graph has been retained in committee files.

[7] German Solar Industry Association, "Statistic Data on the German Solar Power (Photovoltaic) Industry" (April 2014), available at http://www.solarwirtschaft.de/fileadmin/media/pdf/2013_2_BSW-Solar_fact_sheet_solar_power.pdf

[8] Germany Trade and Invest, "German Solar Breaks Three Records Within Two Weeks" (June 18, 2014), available at http://www.gtai.de/GTAI/Navigation/EN/Meta/press,did=1034630.html

[9] U.S. EIA, "EIA Projects Modest Needs for New Electric Generation Capacity" (July 16, 2014), available at http://www.eia.gov/todayinenergy/detail.cfm?id=17131 (summarizing U.S. EIA's projection, in its "Annual Energy Outlook 2014," that 39 GWac of the total 83 GWac of renewables in 2040 would come from solar).

[10] BLM, "Obama Administration Approves Roadmap for Utility-Scale Solar Energy Development on Public Lands" (Oct. 12, 2012), available at http://www.blm.gov/wo/st/en/info/newsroom/2012/october/NR_10_12_2012.html

[11] SEIA, Solar Energy Facts: Q1 2014.

utility-scale solar power plants (see Attachment 2*) stretches across 44 states, from coast to coast.

Solar offers the nation an inexhaustible supply of energy that it can rely on to power the future, while protecting the nation's environment and conservation values. We are grateful for the Committee's support for this emerging, and increasingly important, national asset.

III. Solar and Land Use: Accomplishments & Opportunities

Solar power plants are more efficient than coal in using the nation's land, over the plants' lifetimes, when the generation facility and all of the land needed for fuel are considered.[12] In a June 2013 report, the National Renewable Energy Laboratory (NREL) found that current utility-scale solar technology averages 8.9 acres per MW,[13] meaning that the entire U.S. peak demand[14] could be met with less than 0.3% of the nation's land area. America can count on a small fraction of its valued land to supply the energy it needs well into the future, by using the nation's best solar areas, much of which is located on federal lands, and by supporting solar's continuing innovation, which is certain to increase its efficiency and reduce its land requirements.

Depending on the size of the project, the electricity purchaser, and the goals of the developer, public lands may be attractive for solar power plant siting. The relative complexity of permitting on federal lands, and the overall expense of siting on federal lands relative to private lands, have often led solar developers elsewhere. The vast majority of utility-scale solar projects in the U.S. are built on private lands. Currently, only 23 percent of operating utility-scale solar capacity is located on public lands. Another 1,018 MW of solar power plants are under construction on public lands, comprising 36 percent of all utility-scale megawatts under construction.

In October 2012, the Department of the Interior issued the Record of Decision for the Solar Programmatic Environmental Impact Statement, launching the BLM's Solar Energy Program. The Record of Decision designated 17 areas on BLM-managed lands as priorities for solar development, totaling approximately 285,000 acres. BLM also designated approximately 19 million additional acres that could be made available for solar development through "variance" applications, or through identification of new Solar Energy Zones (two of which have since been established), although far more—nearly 80 million acres of public land—was excluded from solar development.[15] The Solar Energy Program is intended to provide "incentives for development within" the Solar Energy Zones, including "access to existing or planned transmission."[16]

At present, the promised incentives remain a work in progress. Perhaps the most important step that the Department of the Interior could take, working with other federal and state agencies, is to adopt the most successful aspect of the "fast track" renewable energy program applied to renewable energy projects in 2010. That process demonstrated federal and state agencies could promptly and efficiently assess permit applications when working with clear and agreed-upon deadlines, adopting milestone schedules subject to both strategic and tactical oversight as well as corrective action when schedules appeared to slip, and being held accountable to the highest levels of each agency. In the absence of clear deadlines and a high level of commitment, the permitting process cannot attain that high level of effectiveness.

Another effort underway, for which BLM is to be commended, is its regional mitigation program. Piecemeal mitigation undertaken individually by each developer is inefficient, expensive, and less likely to be useful to the species intended to benefit from mitigation than comprehensive solutions. Initial regional mitigation attempts have appeared to be more expensive than other options available to renewable energy developers, and may threaten to provide a disincentive, rather than an incen-

---

* Attachment has been retained in committee files.

[12] Fthenakis & Kim, "Land Use and Electricity Generation: A Life-Cycle Analysis," Renewable and Sustainable Energy Reviews 13, 1465-1474, at p. 1473 (2009).

[13] NREL Land Use Requirements at p.17.

[14] Approximately 768 GW; see U.S. EIA, "Electric Power Annual 2012" (Dec. 2013), Table 8.6.A., "Noncoincident Peak Load by North American Electric Reliability Corporation Assessment Area, 2002 - 2012, Actual," available at http://www.eia.gov/electricity/annual/pdf/epa.pdf.

[15] U.S. Department of the Interior, "Programmatic Environmental Impact Statement for Solar Energy Development in Six Southwestern States ," available at http://www.doi.gov/news/loader.cfm?csModule=security/getfile&pageid=321960

[16] BLM, "Fact Sheet: Renewable Energy: Solar" (updated May 2014), available at http://www.blm.gov/pgdata/etc/medialib/blm/wo/MIN-ERALS_REALTY_AND_RESOURCE_PROTECTION_/energy/solar_and_wind.Par.99571.File.dat/fact_Solar.pdf.

tive, to develop in Solar Energy Zones. Aggregating mitigation requirements should provide economies of scale that decrease costs, and care must be taken to ensure that regional mitigation efforts serve both species and development needs, perhaps by considering use of private land trusts and other innovative means of achieving regional mitigation's multiple goals.

Access to transmission linking solar energy development areas to major electricity demand centers continues to be a gating item for solar development, whether in or outside of Solar Energy Zones. Transmission access to major demand centers is one major factor that differentiates the De Tilla Gulch and Los Mogotes East Solar Energy Zones in Colorado, where BLM's first attempt to hold competitive auctions for solar development failed,[17] from the Dry Lake Solar Energy Zone in Nevada, where BLM's second competitive auction attempt appears to have been successful. Other issues undoubtedly factored into these starkly different results, such as the demand for additional renewable energy in nearby markets, but there can be no doubt that successful solar development requires prompt, reliable permitting of adequate infrastructure, and cannot be successfully developed without it.

SEIA remains engaged with the BLM on the development of the Solar Energy Program and hopeful that the promised incentives for development in Solar Energy Zones—as well as the flexibility to develop in the many prime solar resource areas outside of those zones—will become permanent features of the program.

IV. Making the Most of the Nation's Exceptional Solar Assets: Policy Priorities

As with any industry, and particularly an emerging one, long-term policy certainty is critical to solar achieving its potential. Increased investment, innovation, and deployment are needed for the solar industry to continue to reduce costs and attain its potential as one of the largest contributors to our nation's energy supply. A steady tax policy, providing comparable treatment with other renewable technologies and avoiding "cliff" dates that stop investment cold long before programs actually expire is essential. For this reason, SEIA strongly advocates adoption of a "commence construction" eligibility standard for the solar Investment Tax Credit (ITC).

The ITC has been a major contributor to the rapid growth of the solar industry. In spite of the national economic downturn, solar installations have grown by 3000 percent since the ITC took effect in 2006, a compound annual growth rate of 77 percent. As financers require substantial schedule margins to avoid risk of losing tax benefits, however, the statutory deadline for the ITC is already casting a shadow on solar growth.

To qualify for either the Section 45 Production Tax Credit (PTC) or the Section 48 ITC, all renewable energy facilities had been required to be "placed in service"[18] before a statutory deadline. The American Tax Relief Act of 2012 (ATRA) changed the eligibility standard for certain renewable energy technologies[19] under Section 45 of the tax code, allowing projects using those technologies to qualify for the PTC, so long as the projects "commence construction" prior to the expiration of the tax credit. Notably, this legislation did not encompass solar energy, fuel cells, combined heat and power, or microturbine property. The "commence construction" modification passed in ATRA should be applied to all Section 45 and 48 clean energy incentives, regardless of technology.

Ensuring a consistent "commence construction" trigger for clean energy tax incentives is especially urgent for utility-scale solar projects. Analysis of the dozen largest solar projects expected to be online by 2016 reveals the median time from the early steps of development to commencement of construction is just over three years, and the median time from development to commercial operation is nearly six years. A "commence construction" standard would ease timing pressures on developers by two years or more, pressures that are building now as the ITC deadline looms at the end of 2016. This tax policy improvement would certainly drive the installation of an additional solar capacity that might otherwise not occur.

The Public Land Renewable Energy Development Act of 2013

Stable, appropriate policies encouraging solar deployment on federal lands, such as aspects of the Public Land Renewable Energy Development Act of 2013, if properly implemented, the BLM's Solar Energy Program, are also needed to ensure the

---

[17] Montgomery, "BLM Reloading After Colorado Solar Land Auction No-Shows," Renewable Energy World (Oct. 29, 2013), available at http://www.renewableenergyworld.com/rea/news/article/2013/10/blm-reloading-after-colorado-solar-land-auction-no-shows.

[18] I.e., the facility was required to be complete and capable of generating power substantially equal to its nameplate capacity.

[19] These technologies include wind; open- and closed-loop biomass; geothermal; small irrigation power; municipal solid waste; hydropower; marine and hydrokinetic energy.

nation is making the most of its solar prospects. The commitments and compromises embodied in the Solar Programmatic Environmental Impact Statement process, including enhancing project development prospects in Solar Energy Zones as well as access to other appropriate development areas (referred to as "variance" lands), must be carried through if the nation is to receive the full benefit of its outstanding public solar resources. Permitting improvements for both solar projects and the transmission needed to bring its power to American homes and businesses must be institutionalized if we are to realize solar's potential on public lands.

First, we support the following elements of S. 279:

- Revenue sharing with states and local government.—While solar development provides many net benefits to the communities hosting solar plants, and provides a substantial net environmental benefit overall, no development is without any impact. We agree that a portion of the revenues from solar development on federal lands should be directed to the states and local communities hosting solar power plants, which will help ensure that all fully share in the benefits solar development brings to the nation. We applaud efforts to fund increasing conservation and recreation needs on federal lands, but caution against burdening renewable energy with the costs of doing so, particularly in isolation. To the extent that monies from the solar industry are paid into a conservation fund, care must be taken to account for those contributions when determining the mitigation requirements for solar power plants.
- Improved Permitting Processes.—With appropriate funding and prioritization, the "fast track" projects demonstrated that permitting processes can be timely and effective. High-level interagency coordination across federal and state governments, milestone schedules with clear deadlines, corrective action when necessary, high-level accountability and transparency are all necessary elements to permitting success. The focused funding that S. 279 would potentially make available to institutionalize improved permitting processes is not only appropriate; it is a good investment for improved returns for the public. S. 1397, the Federal Permitting Improvement Act of 2013, while not the subject of today's hearing, seeks to achieve these same goals of transparent milestones, clear deadlines, and agency accountability.

We remain concerned about the certain elements of the Public Lands Renewable Energy Development Act of 2013, including the following aspects, and look forward to working with the sponsors to tailor these provisions to better ensure solar benefits to the nation:

- Competitive Bidding is Counterproductive for an Emerging Industry.—Competitive bidding works best with fully mature industries, where multiple well-established companies can drive costs down by making existing practices more efficient, allowing some of the benefits of those efficiencies to be shared with the landowners-in this case, the federal government. Competitive bidding is not well-suited to an early-stage industry like utility-scale solar, as it encourages incumbent technologies and speculators and discourages the innovation that could ultimately reduce costs for energy customers, increase solar production from federal lands while decreasing land requirements, and provide far greater benefit to the public than could be realized by competitive bidding revenues. Competitive bidding would most likely increase the costs of developing utility-scale solar projects on public lands, and thereby decrease opportunities for innovation that will help make the most of the public lands that are used for renewable energy. Combined with high rental rates, bonds, and other costs, some developers that might have pursued projects on public lands will pursue projects on private lands or not at all.

Recent experience with competitive bidding could not be more varied, with one experiment in Colorado yielding no bidders and a second, in Nevada, yielding apparent success. If competitive bidding is to be pursued, the pilot project approach in the bill is essential to determine whether it can truly work on a sustainable basis, and if so, what factors lead to success or failure. It is essential that any pilot program is not overly prescriptive, allowing the BLM the flexibility to build on success and eliminate factors that deter from it, based on its own analysis as well as feedback from the solar industry. Most importantly, BLM should allow itself the flexibility to continue its current solar permitting regime while any competitive bidding program is evaluated. If the pilot project is considered unsuccessful, BLM should retain the ability to reject the use of competitive bidding and to rely on technical and financial criteria to decide among competing applications.

- Readjustment of Lease Terms Introduces Unfinanceable Risk.—The proposal to open lease terms for renegotiation 15 years into a 25-year lease is simply not financeable. Financers need certainty of sufficient revenues throughout the term of debt financing to ensure repayment. The potential that increased lease costs could eat into revenues by unknown amounts would create unconstrained risk. To ensure financeability of solar power plants and avoid unnecessary risk, which increases costs to electricity consumers, lease terms should remain consistent for the duration of the lease (typically 30 years for a solar right-of-way, which is commensurate with long-duration power purchase agreements).
- Royalties payments.—No royalty payments should be required, regardless of whether competitive bidding is adopted. Solar energy generation does not result in the depletion of the resource, which is the economic rationale for imposing a royalty. Increased solar production from federal lands should be incentivized, not penalized. Royalties charged on an output basis, particularly using a flat percentage, decreases the incremental value to solar developers of maximizing solar generation per acre. Existing rental values for federal lands have already contributed to make those lands less favorable than private lands, and switching to a royalty system could further reduce solar production from federal lands and ultimately provide less, not more, solar revenue for the federal government.

IV. Conclusion

Thank you once again for inviting SEIA to submit this testimony. SEIA is grateful for the tremendous support that solar has across the nation, which is reflected in the great interest and extensive efforts of this Committee. We look forward to working with the Committee to establish the long-term, stable policies needed to make the most of America's exceptional solar assets, delivering solar's benefits to the nation in the form of large quantities of cost-effective, clean and sustainable power, growing numbers of jobs throughout the country, and outstanding economic opportunity.

The CHAIR. Thank you very much.
Mr. Nichols.

STATEMENT OF SCOTT NICHOLS, PERMITTING AND LANDS MANAGER, U.S. GEOTHERMAL, INC.

Mr. NICHOLS. Thank you.

As I have watched this time wind down my mouth has gotten drier, so pardon me if I trip over my tongue.

Madame Chair, Senator Murkowski and members of the committee, first I want to thank you for the knowledge that has been demonstrated by your questions this morning. I am absolutely amazed at your in depth knowledge of the National Environmental Policy Act and the implementation of the rules that go along with our natural resource development.

That said, I am the Manager of Permitting and Lands for U.S. Geothermal. We're a publicly traded, geothermal power company based in Boise, Idaho. We have operations in 3 States, actually 4 States now. We're working on an operation overseas. I've been with the company the last 6 and a half years.

Prior to that I spent over 20 years working cooperatively with the BLM and Forest Service on streamlining permitting at the State level working with staff at both Forest Service and BLM to overlay and implement processes that we felt could shorten up these timeframes and provide the best product available when I was working as a regulator.

What I can tell you is that both of the bills you have here today are outstanding bills, I think. We support those bills. But I wanted to provide a perspective from the logjam side of things and from the renewable energy perspective.

It's not simply money that changes the logjam in permitting. It's also the quality of the decisions that are being made. After spending so many years developing processes what I found is it is not the process that's makes a better decision. It's more specific requirements and the ability to make those decisions that gives our staff the confidence that they can move forward with the decisions they make.

Because right now our staff have lost the technical capability to implement the knowledge they have on the ground. I talked with my friends in the BLM and in the Forest Service day in and day out. I'd like to use a commissioner from my county as a fine example.

She has many, many years of on the ground, day to day experience with the resources in her county. Nobody can replace that. So when we ask biologists to come in and manage wild horses or geothermal resources, who has never been on the ground, they have no history, they have no background. They're relegated to checking a NEPA box to ensure that that box has been checked and that they are free of liability under a lawsuit. That's all it becomes.

If we're going to continue on that path we no longer need people that are experts in the resource to be able to manage the resource. We need people that can check boxes administrators. I don't think that was the intent of the National Environmental Policy Act. It was not the intent of Congress or the House. It's our intent to make good decisions on the ground, but we can't make those good decisions without empowering those individuals to do that.

I've got a minute and 52 seconds and I want to give you an example of the amount of work that goes into the NEPA process for geothermal development.

From the solar industry it sounds like you're working on a programmatic environmental impact statement. The geothermal industry worked on a programmatic environmental impact statement with the BLM. That programmatic EIS identified the lands that were suitable for development. Subsequent to that every district in the Western United States identified the lands that were also suitable for geothermal development. Each of those industries will do the same thing.

Even after two environmental impact statements that are required under Federal regulation to find that there is no opportunity for undue and unnecessary degradation, we still find ourselves bound up in environmental assessments on projects for drilling on a pad that is literally in my discussions this morning with my staff in Nevada, not much bigger than this office, on an existing area where we are currently producing geothermal resources.

So with that background I want to tell you that there are extensive rules in place, extensive rules in place, to support an opportunity for categorical exclusions, streamlining, the ability to make better decisions and empower our BLM staff.

Those are included in the CEQ regulations themselves, 40CFR1500.5.

The Department of Interior's Federal regulations, 43CFR3201 which I just cited with regard to undue and unnecessary degradation.

The Environmental Policy Act of 2005 provides categorical exclusions for oil and gas that have not even been considered for geothermal resources.

BLM's NEPA handbook, 1790–1, provides the categorical exclusions for the forestry industry, the realty industry, for mining, should also be applied to other areas including geothermal. Yet we have staff that are unable to administer those CXs across programs because of administrative concern.

That said, we are working with the Department of Energy on a project in the Santa Medio desert. The Department of Energy recognizes that drilling should be allowed to be conducted within a developed geothermal field. So the Department of Energy is in a situation where they're ready to approve a drill pad, less than one acre in size, that includes no new road building. Yet the BLM has spent over 180 days and $60,000 and more of our company's consulting funds to be able to determine whether we should be able to put a hole in the ground in an existing geothermal producing field.

That said, I want to summarize by saying that streamlined, measureable, performance based requirements is what the industry needs.

Again, I want to go back to the opening statement. It's not better process. It's the ability to make better decisions with the professional staff that we have on the ground. I thank you for your time and I stand for any comments.

[The prepared statement of Mr. Nichols follows:]

PREPARED STATEMENT OF SCOTT NICHOLS, MANAGER OF PERMITTING & LANDS, U.S. GEOTHERMAL INC., ON S. 279 AND S. 2440

Mr. Chairman and members of the Subcommittee, my name is Scott Nichols and I am here today representing U.S. Geothermal Inc. U.S. Geothermal is a publicly traded company that explores for, develops, builds and operates utility scale geothermal power plants. We are a member of the board of directors of the Geothermal Energy Association, a trade association composed of U.S. companies who support the expanded use of geothermal energy and who are developing geothermal resources worldwide for electrical power generation and direct-heat uses. The membership of the Geothermal Energy Association includes large utilities and Independent Power Producers like U.S. Geothermal, equipment suppliers, drilling companies, technical and financial service providers. These companies are primarily focused on the exploration, development and generation of clean, base load electricity from our country's geothermal resource base.

Professionally, I have 28 years of environmental management experience at the state management level, as a consultant and as a corporate environmental and regulatory compliance manager.

My comments are focused on the BLM and USFS (Agencies's) evolving approach in administering the National Environmental Policy Act (NEPA), the geothermal industry's evolving approach to environmental management, and support for action requiring agencies to rigidly defined NEPA implementation and federal regulations.

The NEPA was enacted and implemented as a planning and decision making tool to involve the public in planning and decisions regarding major federal actions significantly affecting the quality of the human environment.[1]

The environmental protection industry learned to utilize the judicial system to expand the scope of the NEPA to include any federal action and decision. At this time all industries and proposals driven by the NEPA process not environmental performance. More paperwork is generated by staff, checklists are completed, and consultants are hired by proponents. Better science is not implemented, requirements are not streamlined, and state efforts are duplicated. Experienced agency field staff with local knowledge and understanding of natural resources are required to document NEPA compliance. Their expertise is replaced by contracted consultants paid for by industry. Agency resources are overloaded by misused environmental policy and process requirements, not by the volume of new industry proposals. This position is supported by the work of state engineers and environmental regulators who can respond to a dynamic development process.

[1] 42 USC § 4331 SEC. 102

The geothermal industry is using environmental baseline evaluations proactively to determine whether an area is suitable for development and to avoid resource conflicts. Unfortunately proactive environmental evaluations and avoidance policy cannot circumvent processes mandated by NEPA. Support for specific exclusions and more defined regulations is found under two existing sections of the BLM's CFR's. 43CFR §3201.11 requires that the BLM will not issue leases for Lands where the Secretary has determined that issuing the lease would cause unnecessary or undue degradation of public lands and resources. 43CFR §3261.12 requires an applicant's operating plan to include the items specified and "you must submit any other information that BLM may require."

Our overwhelming experience is that management decisions are now driven by lawsuits, attorneys and the Office of General Counsel combined with a need for more data and longer evaluation periods. Documentation has become more important than good science. Environmental protection along with healthy plant and animal communities, clean water and air are the basis of our need for renewable energy. In order to accomplish that goal in a reasonable time and under reasonable costs it is incumbent upon our elected leadership to mandate the regulatory changes that will to provide flexibility for renewable energy developments that also provide streamlined, measureable, performance based requirements for out federal resource managers to work within.

The CHAIR. Thank you all very much for that excellent testimony.

Let me begin with a question to each of you. Actually Mr. Nichols got to this question in his testimony, but I want to go ahead and ask it anyway.

What, in addition to increased staff, is necessary to make the process move more smoothly and comprehensively? Not cutting corners, just move more smoothly.

Is it just an increased staff or is it also some of the things that Mr. Nichols said directly and alluded to in his testimony?

How would you answer that question, Mr. Kidwell?

Mr. KIDWELL. I couldn't agree more on a lot of things that Commissioner said, I believe it's Commissioner. I apologize. A lot of the streamlining ideas he had are directly on point and would apply to the oil and gas side too.

In speaking directly, what I can speak to is the Carlsbad field office. What we've seen there as where we've been able to have better process at times is through communication and through working with a State director, who communicates that we're not the bad guy, that we're in this to work together and that going back to something you brought up earlier in your questioning is guiding us and letting us know what, on these permits, on these APDs, you know, we drill a lot of Federal wells out there. We feel like we've got the process down pretty good.

So those types of things, more guidance and that if there's something specific, but I do think it's important the communication that we have and the idea that comes from a State director that we're working together in this and we're not a bad actor, a bad person.

The CHAIR. What would you do in addition to just increase personnel?

Ms. SGAMMA. I think political will. You've got a situation where NEPA is being held up. There's not a will to move that through.

You have a situation where field offices can add requirement on top of requirement on APDs so that packet never gets completed.

You've got a situation where leasing is often just deferred indefinitely because a field manager or the State office doesn't want to face controversy. They know they're not going to get support from Washington.

So I think political will is big element.

The CHAIR. Commissioner.

Mr. CHRISTENSEN. Madame Chair, I would like to bring two things to point.

One, as I noted earlier, we are down from a 3,000 well backlog that we saw in 2003. We're now at 156 conventional and 59 CBM permits.

The thing I'd like to add though is that I think some of it has to do with terminology. So BLM tells us that the time that they use is 9 days. Nine days is the time it takes to turn around an APD. That is specifically timed once the APD is considered complete.

What we are told, though, was from notice of survey to completion it's 300 days. That's for our local Buffalo field office.

The CHAIR. Right. This committee, look, I went through this nightmare after the Mercando spill so I am not an expert yet. But I am extremely knowledgeable about the different characterizations of when a permit is pending, when it starts, etcetera.

We're going to put it on a sheet of paper from the time somebody expresses an interest in drilling until the end. We're going to see what that backlog actually is. We're not going to be confused with just different terminologies. That's what happened to us in the Gulf of Mexico.

So I have some sympathy with this. We're going to work with the agency very carefully because waiting a couple of years is not—capital can go anywhere these days. It will. It will go to other counties. It will go to other places. It will go to other countries. It is not going to wait for inefficient government processes.

So I'm, you know, not coming to any hard, you know, final here. But thank you, yes. We're going to lay that process out in writing.

But go ahead. I didn't want to interrupt you. Go ahead and finish your thought.

Mr. CHRISTENSEN. I think some of that, as you were saying too, as was mentioned beside me, is political will. Where we are we have a very good relationship with the Buffalo field office. But unfortunately they answer to people up above them. They also receive feedback from Washington.

The thing I would add as well is that Campbell County has been fortunate now. But if you would have looked to Park County which is where Cody, Wyoming is, they've had APDs deferred for almost 5 years. Some of that's been waiting on a RMP revision. But unfortunately what happens when you have 5 years of deferrals is the capital has left Park County.

The CHAIR. Yes, absolutely.

Mr. CHRISTENSEN. Yes.

The CHAIR. The people just cannot wait that long.

Mr. CHRISTENSEN. They have noticed a decrease in assessment.

The CHAIR. Let's go, real quick.

What else, in addition to staffing, what would you say? In addition to more personnel, what would be needed?

Ms. WICHMAN. Political capital was the nice or the political will to make something happen was a nice way to put it. But it's, from my perspective and what I've seen, is that it's much easier on in our local field offices for them to put off making decisions by stating something is incomplete simply because they have a—they're managing the resource for the judicial system. They're not managing the resource for the sake of the resource or the folks who live there.

As a very brief example, we filed for a permit on a road that had been maintained and managed by the county for 40 years. We had to pay for and wait for the archeological survey.

The CHAIR. OK.

Next, real quickly then I've got to turn to my colleagues.

Mr. HAUBENSTOCK. Sure.

Chair Landrieu, I think you're on exactly the right track when you talked about laying things out on a sheet of paper.

If we look at what's worked in the past you can't manage what you don't measure. What has really worked well is putting things on a dashboard.

Identifying what the deadlines are.

Identifying milestone schedules to get there.

Having corrective action when things fall off.

Having the transparency and accountability that a dashboard provides.

Another idea is to have an ombudsperson. That has worked very, very well in the past, someone who can see through all the different issues that are coming up and guide developers through to success.

The CHAIR. Thank you.

Mr. Nichols, if you don't mind holding because your testimony was basically an answer to that question. I'm going to turn to Senator Murkowski.

Then I have one more question about revenue sharing to the local counties, but let me recognize my Ranking Member.

Senator MURKOWSKI. Thank you, Madame Chairman.

I think the comments that we've received from you all have been very helpful because I think what we're trying to do here is not just vent and say we've got a problem. But what are some of the potential solutions here. I think we've gotten some good proposals.

Mr. Nichols, you talked about the quality of decisions. But I think we also recognize that a lot of times that means you've got to have quality people that actually know what it is that they are processing, that have some familiarity, as you used in your example.

I think sometimes within our agencies that presents a challenge because the real knowledgeable folks get scooped up by industry. They get scooped up by others who are able to pay them more. Mr. Concho probably, or excuse me, Mr. Kidwell probably has some of them working for him at Concho there.

But the issue that you raise, just briefly here, Mr. Haubenstock, about the accountability because I think you suggested that sometimes when you don't have the political will it's just easier to defer, delay. If there's no accountability for a timely decision, if you can just continue, kind of, putting it off, putting it off. Sometimes folks give up.

That's certainly what we've seen in Alaska. After a while it seems like the agency is just trying to wait you out or kind of a slow bleed. Eventually you give up. That's not the goal here.

Mr. Kidwell, I wanted to ask you with your experience there in New Mexico. I think you indicated that in terms of the permits and I believe this was on the Federal lands back in 2011 you said 80 days. Now we're up to 133 days. Is that what I understood correctly?

Mr. KIDWELL. That's correct, Senator. 133 is our average. That's a Concho specific average of 133 days.

Senator MURKOWSKI. OK.

Mr. KIDWELL. Up from 80 days in 2011.

Senator MURKOWSKI. How does that compare with the timeliness of getting a lease or a permit from the State of New Mexico?

Mr. KIDWELL. With regard to the State of New Mexico we're able to get a permit within anywhere from 3 days to 2 weeks at a far end.

Senator MURKOWSKI. So 3 days to 2 weeks verses 133 days?

Tell me why, if this is all in the Permian Basin there in New Mexico and you've indicated it's a pretty prolific field and the resource is great there.

Tell me why you would even choose to pursue leasing on Federal lands, on our public lands, when you can move to exploration production and making money on State lands within a couple weeks?

Mr. KIDWELL. Yes.

No, that's a great question, Senator. Obviously, we do. We have a lot of State lands also.

But as you look at the Permian Basin what we're dealing with there is two counties, Eddy and Lee County, New Mexico, is where the Permian Basin, essentially is. So you've got a lot of Federal lands there.

Senator MURKOWSKI. Alright.

Mr. KIDWELL. It's such a productive basin, obviously, a lot of this resource is covered by Federal BLM lands. So as we look to develop that resource we're, kind of, you know, going to have to develop BLM lands.

Obviously if you're sitting there looking at it and a lot of factors going into make a decision as to whether you're going to drill a well. The timing factor is certainly is one of those. I mean if I could go here, if I've got an opportunity to drill two sections over in 2 weeks, in 3 weeks, you know, in a much faster timeframe, obviously that's going to be something that's appealing.

But because of the amount of resource potential that we see and have experienced and is there, we, kind of, deal with what we have to deal with. That's why I think it's, this bill, is so important that we bring people in there. It's a focused bill, as you know, to bring specific people and address this specific issue of bringing those time periods down.

So we can go develop the resource that's——

Senator MURKOWSKI. Would you all agree that the discussion that we were having with Director Kornze earlier about what we're seeing in terms of increases or decreased productivity on our public lands? Would you all concur that a part of what we're seeing with the decline is this disparity with how quickly you can move on State and private lands verses the delays on Federal lands?

Ms. SGAMMA. Absolutely, yes.

Our members will, you know, go to the State and private lands and only to Federal lands when they have to you when, you know, it's just part of the lease hold. You can't avoid it in the West.

Senator MURKOWSKI. Mr. Nichols.

Mr. NICHOLS. With geothermal operations also we selectively target private lands and that BLM lands are a last resort.

Senator MURKOWSKI. Last resort.

Mr. Haubenstock.

Mr. HAUBENSTOCK. For solar as well what we have seen is that solar developers will go to private land instead of public land because it is much more complex, timely and expensive to go on Federal land. There's a promise of improvements and we're looking forward to seeing those improvements made concrete.

Senator MURKOWSKI. We'd like to make some improvements here.

Thank you.

The CHAIR. Senator Barrasso, thank you for being a part of this important hearing.

Senator BARRASSO. Thank you, Madame Chairman.

I appreciate it.

Commissioner Christensen, in your testimony you said that delays in the timely permitting of oil and gas wells makes States with Federal lands less attractive for development. You explained the energy companies within our State and in your county, they compete with capital within other divisions across the United States. You go on to say that energy companies know that if they can't get a timely permit in Wyoming they're just going to someplace else.

For this reason you say that timely approval is critical to the long term health and prosperity of the citizens of our communities in terms of the impacts.

So I just wanted to visit with you a little bit as a County Commissioner and ask if you'd maybe discuss in greater detail how these delays in approving the oil and gas permits, how it impacts communities with significant amounts of Federal land?

Mr. CHRISTENSEN. Thank you, Senator Barrasso.

It's actually, it's a multi tiered piece. To provide a little bit of background on the way that revenues work in Campbell County, for example.

The county collects ad valorem taxes on natural resource production. Unfortunately those revenues come in 16 months after the production itself happens. So if you're in a county you're seeing the impacts of the production up front before you're seeing the revenue.

You have to make decisions related to infrastructure improvements, roadways, hospital expansions, schools, any number of other things, almost on a hunch, that these permits are going to continue to be turned around quickly and that you're going to continue to see revenue.

It's the same thing for the companies that operate where we do. Unlike much of Wyoming, Campbell County is fortunate because 92 percent or a little over 80 percent of our surface is private. But because of the split estate issues within Campbell County, you see over 90 percent of the mineral estate being BLM.

So what happens is is through control of that mineral estate BLM drives the issues on the surface. It adds to the complexity and adds to the time.

When we look at the issues for the community as well what you see when you have this kind of development is you have people who come in, they move. If you want to make your community attractive and basically advance it from, like, a commuter community, you have to invest in quality of life.

The only way to invest in quality of life is to know that those revenues are going to be there long term.

Senator BARRASSO. So it's a budget impact in terms of roads, hospitals, schools. It has a man power impact in terms of from a community level, law enforcement, EMTs, fire fighters and also a work force issue related to the companies and their hiring patterns and housing, I'd imagine.

Mr. CHRISTENSEN. I would agree.

One of the things that we're actually fortunate, we're undergoing a bit of an oil boom right now. Fortunately the community is in a better position to handle it than it was during the methane gas.

When methane gas happened Gillette's town that went from about 25,000 people to 35,000 people in 4 years and you have huge growth. You have huge infrastructure needs. Like I said, it takes a while for that revenue to catch up with the infrastructure demand.

Unfortunately the methane gas fell off as we see the shale plays and the natural gas development. Methane isn't cost effective to produce.

The thing that is helping the community this time around is the fact that a lot of those workers who were there for methane gas are going back to work for oil and gas. Without that certainty it makes it difficult for those companies and for those workers to have a good, long term, sustained presence in your community.

Senator BARRASSO. OK.

Ms. Sgamma, in your testimony you encouraged the committee to act quickly on S. 2440. As you said, your organization has heard reports from busy BLM field offices that they're already starting to feel a pinch of the impending September 2015 deadline. I think you say that the field managers can't hire replacements to handle the workloads because they don't know whether the funding for those hires will continue beyond that 2015 date.

Will you just expand a little bit upon why it's important that Congress reauthorize the permitting program this year?

Ms. SGAMMA. I think it's for that reason is that, you know, it might be a deadline in 2015, but it's causing effects today in 2014. If that funding, you know, if there's no certainty that that funding is going to come in then I don't think we're going to see those BLM offices staff up.

Senator BARRASSO. I think you also said that targeting the funds more directly to the BLM field offices is important to your alliance members, making sure the money actually goes where it's supposed to go. Is it fair to say your members wouldn't be supporting any kind of higher permit fees if the bill directed revenues, say, just to the Department of the Treasury?

Ms. SGAMMA. Absolutely correct, yes.

Senator BARRASSO. Thank you, Madame Chairman.

The CHAIR. Thank you.

Let me just wrap up with this question to Campbell County.

How do you share in revenues? We understand how Wyoming happily shares its partnership with the Federal Government. Many of our Western States have about a 50/50 split. That's not the same situation, sadly, for coastal States which we're trying to rectify.

But how does Wyoming share with Campbell County? Do you all have a split of revenues at the County level?

Mr. CHRISTENSEN. We're fortunate in—and I'll honestly tell you I've been looking at other States. I think the Wyoming model, we're very fortunate in the way that it works.

The State assesses a severance tax when the mineral is extracted. That's paid monthly.

The County then assesses an ad valorem tax with the property taxes the following year.

That's where I say in that for us, the revenue may be up to 16 months delayed.

In that particular case, we assess at a mill against it at market value and——

The CHAIR. OK, so you all assess an additional ad valorem tax. You don't share directly in the State of Wyoming's revenue.

In other words they don't send back to the counties a portion of the severance royalties, etcetera, etcetera?

Mr. CHRISTENSEN. They do not directly.

The CHAIR. Directly.

But you get the ad valorem increase?

Mr. CHRISTENSEN. We do.

Now the one thing that does happen is the Governor and the legislature does do direct distribution. Those are moneys from the general fund which go directly to county and municipal government.

The other thing is that——

The CHAIR. Is it based on production or is it a formula that drives it otherwise?

Mr. CHRISTENSEN. It's actually, it's based on politics.

[Laughter.]

Mr. CHRISTENSEN. So——

The CHAIR. Which we are familiar with that on this committee. But——

Mr. CHRISTENSEN. Which means that there is a complicated formula based on population, an inverse of assessed valuation and then a number of other things to offset.

The CHAIR. But it's not directly related to production?

Mr. CHRISTENSEN. No.

The one exception is there is a program through the slip board which will approve funds that is directly for energy impacted communities. That is something that the State has put in place knowing that these communities have major impacts and they will help you, basically, get started until you start to see those revenues come in.

The CHAIR. OK.

I think this has been an excellent panel. We've exceeded our time slightly, but with our recess I think we're right on time.

But let me just say that the Ranking Member and I are very committed to increasing the production of all the above, solar, wind, geothermal and traditional production on Federal land and balance it with the environmental needs, generating some additional funding for the Federal Government, but also making sure that the counties that serve as hosts for the productions are fairly treated, not only by the Federal Government but I think, also by their host States.

So we, you know, if somewhat limited reach as between the States and the counties. But we can have some influence. I think it is important for the government to understand that the revenues that are generated are being generated at very local levels and they need schools, hospitals, sewer systems, roads.

Senator Murkowski struggles with that in Alaska with a population that's sometimes sparse. We struggle with that in Louisiana along our coast as well.

So your testimony has really been very timely. Thank you all very much.

The record will stay open for 2 weeks. Additional testimony is welcome.

We do look forward to moving these bills forward as soon as we can.

Thank you all very much.

Meeting adjourned.

[Whereupon, at 4:45 p.m. the hearing was adjourned.]

APPENDIXES

APPENDIX I

Responses to Additional Questions

WESTERN ENERGY ALLIANCE,
Denver, CO, August 18, 2014.

Hon. MARY LANDRIEU,
U.S. Senate Committee on Energy and Natural Resources, Washington, DC.

DEAR CHAIRMAN LANDRIEU: Thank you for the opportunity to appear before your committee for the hearing to understand the obstacles to permitting energy projects on federal lands and S.2440, the BLM Permit Processing Improvement Act of 2014.

I also appreciate the chance to respond to questions; my answers to questions from committee members are attached. Given the confusion on the oil and natural gas production numbers discussed during the hearing and permit processing times, I would ask that the attached documents are included in the record for the hearing:

- The Congressional Research Service report U.S. Crude Oil and Natural Gas Production in Federal and Non-Federal Areas. The report documents the federal production numbers, but also puts those in context with non-federal production. The report shows a declining federal percentage.
- An analysis from Norton Rose Fulbright of BLM permitting times. Using data obtained from a FOIA request, Norton attorney Poe Leggette describes how BLM tracking of permitting times is wildly inconsistent, rendering BLM assessments of how long it takes to process a permit inaccurate: "By exaggerating 'Industry' days, BLM deflects responsibility for slow processing."

Thank you again for including Western Energy Alliance in the hearing, and for the ability to provide follow-up information.

Sincerely,

KATHLEEN M. SGAMMA,
Vice President of Government & Public Affairs.

[Enclosure.]

RESPONSE TO QUESTION FROM SENATOR MURKOWSKI

Question 1. Ms. Sgamma, you said something in your testimony that got my attention. You testified that S. 2440 is only a partial solution to addressing the barriers to production on federal lands. In your view, what are other steps we can take to enhance production on federal lands?

Answer. S.2440 is only a partial solution because it only addresses one stage of the three stage onshore process. Looking very broadly at the steps required to develop oil and natural gas on federal lands, there are three main processes: leasing, environmental analysis under the National Environmental Policy Act (NEPA), and permitting. There are currently many impediments and bureaucratic inefficiencies in all three main processes, while S. 2440 addresses only a subset of one phase of the federal onshore process. See the attached chart which shows the length of time it can take from leasing through to production.

PHASE 1 LEASING

Currently it can take many years for leases to become available. An operator starts by doing some exploratory work, determines what areas may be prospective for oil and/or natural gas, and attempts to put a leasehold together, which often consists of a mixture of private, state and federal lands. After the company submits a nomination for a federal parcel, it may wait years before that land is offered at a lease sale. Meanwhile, they develop on adjacent private and state lands, and the American taxpayer loses revenue from federal royalties. Other indications of leasing delays include:

- Since the leasing policy changes in 2010, leasing times have lengthened significantly. Wyoming reports for example that the time from nomination to lease sale extended from three to six months to 12 to 18 months after the 2010 policy changes.
- 2013 marked a new low for BLM. The 1.17 million acres leases issued that year were the lowest on record. The record dates back to 1988.
- BLM Director Neil Kornze claimed in his testimony that because industry did not bid on all the acreage it offered, then BLM is ahead of industry demand. Rather, this may indicate that BLM is offering leases that companies are either no longer interested in after waiting for years, or the leases may have such onerous restrictions placed on them that companies cannot economically develop those leases.
- Also, the fact that some acreage is offered but not bid on does not erase the fact that there are millions of acres that companies are interested in that is not offered for sale. For example, in the West in 2013, 2,661 parcels were nominated by companies, but 1,416 (53%) were deferred. Once a parcel is deferred it is generally deferred indefinitely, often for years.

PHASE 2 NEPA ANALYSIS

In the NEPA phase, inefficiencies and bureaucratic delays are also readily apparent. Since 2009, this Administration has approved only three major oil and natural gas projects on federal lands: the West Tavaputs, Greater Natural Buttes and Gasco Natural Gas projects. Western Energy Alliance tracks the outstanding major project NEPA that is awaiting government action, using a study from SWCA Environmental Consultants. Outstanding NEPA analyses of over three years duration represent 2,055 potential wells annually which could provide nearly 79,000 jobs and $17.8 billion in annual economic impact. Some of the projects have been held up in the NEPA process for over eight years.

Meanwhile, several other major projects are indefinitely stalled, and even minor Environmental Assessments for small numbers of wells can take many years. Small companies often wait four years for NEPA approval of small projects, often of just ten wells.

PHASE 3 PERMITTING

After the NEPA documentation is approved, a company can finally submit an Application for Permit to Drill (APD). S.2440 provides funding for this phase, but does not take care of problems inherent in the APD phase. For example, despite statutes requiring permits to be handled within thirty days, BLM claims to take 194 days on average to process a permit. For various reasons, we believe that number is not accurate (see the analysis from Norton Rose Fulbright of BLM permitting times), yet even given that it is a low estimate, it is considerably more than state processing times. Providing funding is not a guarantee that the timelines will improve.

Another problem at the permitting stage is that several field offices are requiring companies to undergo additional analysis which are not required by law or policy. These ad hoc requirements add considerably to APD processing times. BLM will often attribute that processing time to the companies, even though BLM is adding to the timeframe. Our members have been required to conduct additional wildlife, cultural, floodplain, and other analyses beyond what is required by regulation or policy. S.2440 will not change that situation; only better management, adherence to statute and policy, and political will will correct those additional bureaucratic inefficiencies.

However, despite the fact that S.2440 is only a partial solution, it is a critical one. Without adequate funding, we can almost guarantee that permitting times will increase. Western Energy Alliance would rather see incremental steps taken to support efficient APD processing, rather than wait for one solution that fixes everything.

RESPONSES TO QUESTIONS FROM SENATOR BARRASSO

Question 1. In his testimony, Mr. Kornze states that:

"[l]ast year, the BLM held 30 separate oil and gas lease sales, offering 5.7 million acres for lease by industry, the most in a decade; industry submitted bids on fewer than one-in-five of these acres."

A. I understand that of the 5.7 million acres offered for lease in FY 2013, about 1.2 million acres were leased in the lower 48 and 4.5 million acres were offered in Alaska's National Petroleum Reserve. Is that correct?

Answer. Yes. The source of these data is a spreadsheet with offered and sold parcels for FY 2009 to 2013.

B. I understand that the 1,172,808 issued in the lower 48 in FY 2013 was the smallest number of issued in the lower 48 since FY 1988, the last year of available data. Is that correct?

Answer. Yes with the refinement that the source of these numbers is the "number of acres leased spreadsheet" which should more correctly be labeled "number of acres issued." I am only aware of one consolidated source of offered and sold data from BLM, and that data set only covers FY 2009 to 2013, so it is not the source for statement B.

Again, the incomplete data have caused confusion. BLM's imprecise use of the term "leased" and the fact that the numbers hover around 1.2 million for both issued and offered acres may be the source of confusion. The number of acres issued by BLM in 2013 was 1,172,808, but the acreage offered was 1,282,320. Some acreage offered in years prior to 2013 was invariably included in the amount issued in 2013, and some offered in 2013 had not yet been issued in 2013.

C. I understand that industry submitted bids on approximately 65 percent of the 1.2 million acres offered for lease in the lower 48 in FY 2013. Is that correct?

Answer. Yes. Of the 1,282,320 acres offered in the lower 48, bids were received on 836,673 acres. As Western Energy Alliance covers oil and natural gas issues for the lower 48 and Alaska's circumstances and regulations differ quite a bit from those in the lower 48, I cannot offer insight into why BLM offered so much acreage in Alaska with such little interest from industry. However, I do know that Mr. Kornze lumped the acreage together in his testimony to try to make the case that BLM is far ahead of industry demand. His contention certainly does not apply to the lower 48, and in fact BLM continues to defer millions of acres across the West that industry has nominated, but BLM will not bring up for sale. Offering millions of acres in Alaska that is of little interest to Alaskan producers doesn't compensate for the fact that there are millions of acres that western producers cannot lease because of indefinite deferrals. In fact, of the 2,661 parcels nominated in 2013, 53% were deferred, or 1,416. That does not include the backlog of parcels nominated in prior years that have yet to be offered.

The statements are generally correct with the following refinement. Because of incomplete data and imprecise use of terms in BLM's released statistics, there seems to be some slight confusion.

On BLM's main oil and gas statistics page is a chart entitled "Number of Acres Leased During the Fiscal Year." "Leased" is an imprecise term. As far as we can tell, this chart refers to acres issued during the fiscal year. Since leases are often sold in one fiscal year but not issued until another, it would be better if BLM released standard charts with all of the following lease points for both numbers of parcels and acres:

- Nominated-lands are not considered for leasing until someone expresses interest by nominating parcels.
- Considered-BLM conducts a leasing Environmental Assessment (EA), including a public comment period, for a subset of nominated parcels.
- Posted-BLM then decides from those parcels analyzed in the leasing EA which ones it will post for sale, and issues a formal sale notice. The sale notice has all the potential parcels that will be considered for inclusion in an upcoming state sale.
- Protested-After the sales notice is issued, a public comment period commences. Often individuals or groups will protest the inclusion of specific parcels for an upcoming sale.
- Deferred-Based on the protests, BLM will often pull parcels from the sales list, deferring them until some future date. We find that it is often years before deferred parcels will be noticed for sale again.
- Offered-After the initial parcel list is winnowed down, usually a smaller subset from the original sales notice are actually offered at a lease sale.

- Sold-Parcels actually receiving bids at the lease sale or via the post-sale non-competitive process.
- Issued-Once BLM receives the bonus bids and first year's rental for the sold parcels, it can issue the leases. There is usually a minimum of sixty days after sale until a lease is issued, but there are many cases where it is years until parcels are issued.

Having all these data points gives the complete picture of the leasing process, and only with all these points can solid conclusions be drawn about the leasing process. I've offered some refinements to the statements in the question based on my understanding of the limited data BLM has released publicly.

Question 2. In his testimony, Mr. Kornze stated:

> "Industry now has nearly 7,000 approved drilling permits that are ready for drilling but currently sitting unused. If you compare that figure against the fact that an average of about 3,000 wells are spud on public lands each year, it becomes apparent that industry has ample opportunities to develop leased resources."

How do you respond to Mr. Kornze's statement?

Answer. Generally, we heard in Director Kornze's testimony that all is well in the onshore oil and natural gas program and BLM is staying ahead of market demand. BLM offers statistics to support that view, but its selective release of statistics tells only one side of the story and papers over vast inefficiencies in the system. I believe Chair Landrieu's frustration with trying to understand the selective production statistics discussed during the hearing is indicative of the general frustration industry also faces. The current Administration has implemented policies to slow oil and natural gas development on federal lands, but then masks the true effects of those policies by releasing those statistics that appear to support its contention that BLM is supporting development. BLM also selectively releases statistics that attempt to point the finger at producers as the sources of the problem, accusing companies of not using permits or producing on leased acreage.

Fewer bureaucratic obstacles would lead to more efficient development on federal lands and more production. Instead, we've seen a decrease on federal lands, absolutely in the case of natural gas and relatively with oil, and producers are extremely frustrated with the system. BLM's attempts to gloss over those real concerns are not helpful, when in fact inefficiencies in the bureaucracy cause distortions in the system not seen on non-federal lands. For example, because producers have no certainty on how long it will take to get a BLM APD approved, they must submit many more APDs in advance than they may actually use in the hopes that some will make it through the system in time for them to develop. Producers must have enough permits in hand to stay ahead of their rigs, because idle rigs are extremely costly. Producers are attempting to avoid a situation of having to lay down a rig because they cannot get approved permits from BLM.

As a result, there are permits in the federal system that may go unused for long periods of time, a situation not observed on non-federal lands. Since producers know how long a state permit takes, generally around thirty days on average, they do not have to try to anticipate years in advance how many permits they need and stockpile them as they must with federal permits.

BLM Director Kornze mentioned that about 7,000 permits have been approved but not drilled. (BLM statistics show that number is actually 6,711 as of September 2013, the most recent data released by BLM.) Companies would not have to stockpile permits if there were more regulatory certainty on the timeframe for receiving those permits, but it is not uncommon to have to wait two years or more for a permit. Once an initial well is drilled, the producer may determine that the area is not as productive as originally thought, and may decide that the additional permits that it had obtained for adjacent wells are not worth drilling. Since producers know the length of time it takes to obtain a state permit, there is no need to stockpile permits for non-federal lands in advance.

Market conditions may also change years later from the original APD submission. Many permits for natural gas lie unused because there came to be a glut of natural gas in the U.S. Many of those permits may not be drilled until demand again increases for natural gas. In a more efficient system, such as on non-federal lands, producers would not have to have obtained those permits years in advance, and there would not be such as large stock of unused permits. But the inefficiencies in the federal system compel that stockpiling. Furthermore, the fact that there are unused natural gas permits does not mean that there are not plenty of producers waiting for permits for oil wells, some delayed years.

RESPONSE OF COMMISSIONER LORINDA WICHMAN TO QUESTION FROM SENATOR MURKOWSKI

Question 1. In your testimony you state that "the current practices and permitting processes to reach our resources have discouraged many from pursuing projects on federally managed lands." Could you give some examples? To what extent does the legislation address those challenges?

Answer. Prior to the introduction and hope of passage of S.2440 there have been O&G parcels offered in Railroad Valley, Nye County, Nevada. During conversations with perspective producers I have been told the cost and time involved to meet all the permitting requirements have rendered projects economically unattainable.

Since the introduction of S.2440, Nye County has seen an increase in successful BLM O&G lease auctions, as recently as June of this year.

That is my personal observation as it relates to O&G leases. I am hoping that this legislation will provide a process that can be duplicated in other areas of disposal or permitting on BLM managed lands.

In May of 2010, I completed an application for a R&PP lease of a historically significant community cemetery in Manhattan, NV. It was nearly a year later when I received the first response to my application in which it was suggested that I apply for a direct sale to avoid the reversionary clause of the R&PP patent. So Nye County did as requested and applied for a direct sale. The paperwork was completed in August of 2011. Yesterday August 5, 2014 the board of county commissioners approved an offer for sale of the cemetery and approved the purchase for $6,500.

I shake my head while wondering how much of the tax payers money was spent in the last four years and three months to finalize a sale of 7.5 acres at $6,500.

With time I can gather specific examples as it relates to renewable energy projects, mineral exploration and geothermal projects however at this moment they would only be antidotal.

RESPONSES OF MARK A. CHRISTENSEN TO QUESTIONS FROM SENATOR MURKOWSKI

Question 1. What is the typical APD backlog at Wyoming offices today? What do expect it would be if you did not have this program in place?

Answer. The Bureau of Land Management in Wyoming is comprised of three (3) Districts and ten (10) Field Offices. As of today, there are 898 pending applications for permits to drill (APDs). The volume of APDs is significantly higher in the Field Offices located adjacent to energy development areas in the State. The Casper, Buffalo and Pinedale Offices account for ninety percent (90%) of the current pending APDs.

Two (2) Field Offices in Wyoming were selected to participate in the BLM Pilot Project Program: Buffalo and Rawlins. If the pilot project program were not in place, the additional Staffing Team to process the APDs would not exist and the impact would be considerable. As reported in my earlier testimony, at the height of the Coal Bed Methane (CBM) boom the Buffalo Field Office alone had 3,000 pending APDs. Once an Office gets behind, it is very difficult to catch up. Representative Lummis took the lead in the past year to successfully allow for pilot project funding to be re-directed from the Buffalo Field Office to the Casper Field Office, thereby averting the potential for an unmanageable number of APDs to accumulate and managing the resources wisely.

Question 2. You testified that in the Buffalo field office, it takes approximately 300 days from the Notice of Survey to when a permit to drill is issued. In addition to the benefits the pilot program is providing, what are some other examples of ways to expedite the processing of an APD?

Answer. The achievements of the pilot project program for Wyoming and specifically the Buffalo Field Office have been substantial. The ongoing keys to success are: retention of the seasoned personnel facilitating the APDs, insuring applications initially submitted are complete and accurate, addressing all deficiencies promptly, on-site inspections are conducted in a timely manner and cooperatively with the Operator, adhering to schedules and sustaining effective communication between all parties. The complexity of the current APD's is much greater than with the previous CBM wells, necessitating a more thorough understanding of the environmental, archaeological and engineering aspects of each drilling permit. It is also important to acknowledge the immense area for which the Buffalo Field Office is responsible; the three (3) counties of Campbell, Johnson and Sheridan include over 11,500 square miles.

RESPONSES OF SCOTT NICHOLS TO QUESTIONS FROM SENATOR MURKOWSKI

Question 1. What specific regulatory changes would you recommend be made to improve access to geothermal energy?

Answer. The regulatory changes necessary to improve access to geothermal energy are associated with geothermal lease auctions and drilling application standards of the federal regulations, 43 CFR 3200.

1) We believe the federal geothermal lease program should be amended to incentivize private exploration and reduce speculative leasing. The current requirement to limit the initial offer of geothermal lands only by way of a competitive bid inhibits private exploration. When local and regional BLM planning documents include geothermal development scenarios the land that agency staff has not listed for competitive lease should be open and available for non-competitive leasing at a premium rent.

2) The federal regulations governing geothermal operation plans and review should be amended to reduce ambiguity and establish performance based application, review, and approval standards. The amendments should also include a time period for agency review and automatic approval if staff is unable to respond. The backlog of permit applications and extended review periods are the result of personal interpretation and biases of internal resource specialists (wild horses, wildlife, range, recreation) not the review ability of the agency's engineer. Performance based requirements and reducing ambiguity provides regulatory certainty and legal protection.

Question 2. Given your experience, do you have any suggestions on how we might implement NEPA?

Answer. Our suggestions are related to NEPA implementation and include eliminating the need for multiple NEPA analyses on the same project, development of appropriate categorical exclusions and the designation of geothermal NEPA analysis team.

1) At least three independent NEPA analyses are currently completed for a geothermal project. Multiple decision points create uncertainty and delay funding. If the BLM has conducted a NEPA analysis for leasing and issued a Finding of No Significant Impact, subsequent development activity should be exempt from further NEPA review. All subsequent operations should be administered under performance based regulations (as previously discussed) and exempt from further NEPA review.

2) Geothermal resource exploration is one of the most "environmentally friendly" natural resource developments that can be proposed; yet, the proposed activities are scrutinized in more detail than most other land use activities with greater consequences. A new list of geothermal categorical exclusions should be developed for the industry. A comprehensive list of categorically excluded activities would promote exploration and reduce development times.

3) Many BLM offices are subject to high staff turnover that prevent resource experts from learning the unique resource characteristics of the Field Office. We recommend the development of a geothermal NEPA compliance team. A dedicated geothermal NEPA team would establish intrastate and interstate knowledge of the resource and provide consistent assessments of resource impacts. A dedicated NEPA team would build the technical expertise to provide consistently defensible Assessments. Finally, individual projects would be less susceptible to local bias and personal staff agendas.

Thank you for the opportunity to provide additional comments and recommendations regarding the Bureau of Land Management's regulatory programs and NEPA implementation.

––––––

RESPONSES OF ARTHUR HAUBENSTOCK TO QUESTIONS FROM

Question 1. What is the most significant difference between seeking to build utility scale power plants on public lands and private lands in terms of permitting and other government requirements?

Answer. The most significant difference between building a utility-scale power plant on public lands, rather than private lands, is ultimately the cost—in significant part, because time is money, particularly for project developers. The cost difference is evidenced in several different ways. First, the process through which a developer obtains a permit to access and build a power plant on the land is typically much longer in the federal process versus a state or private land process. The increased amount of time spent on the permit translates directly into an increased expenditure of funds by the developer, as well as lost opportunity costs. In other words, the developer could have been building more projects in that time, providing greater contributions to national renewable energy goals, and enabling them to earn more revenue in the same amount of time. While the BLM has proven that it can act quickly in processing solar project approvals, as it did with the projects potentially qualifying for ARRA benefits, it has not maintained that pace nor fully institutionalized systems that could achieve consistent, prompt results. BLM did issue Environmental Assessments for the projects located within the Dry Lake Solar Energy Zone promptly, and should be commended for that, but it should be recognized that the Environmental Impact Statement those recent documents "tiered" from took approximately four years to complete. By adopting consistent approval milestones, clear dashboards for assessing progress, and corrective action when approvals fall behind schedule, BLM can significantly improve its processes.

Second, the annual rents, annual capacity fee payments, and bonus bids collected by the BLM are often greater than the leasing fees a developer would pay to a private landowner, and ultimately may be a greater than the cost of acquiring the land outright. Once the project is running, ongoing efforts to monitor the site for unanticipated impacts can prove to be more costly on federal lands, and the risk that BLM will require additional mitigation measures adds costs to financing projects due to uncertainty in addition to whatever the direct mitigation costs may be. Finally, BLM requires expensive, up-front posting of costs for restoration of the lands (this is in addition to the mitigation for the use of the lands), unlike most private land arrangements.

[Responses to the following questions were not received at the time the hearing went to press:]

QUESTION FOR NEIL KORNZE FROM SENATOR LANDRIEU

Question 1. If S. 279 was enacted into law, a royalty would be assessed for the first time on solar and wind development on public land. In this scenario, would you be supportive of the sharing of revenues from Federal resources, so that counties get some piece of the economic development that is occurring? Also, in this scenario, would you be supportive of a portion of the revenue sharing being directed to go toward the restoration of those areas impacted by development?

QUESTION FOR NEIL KORNZE FROM SENATOR MARK UDALL

Question 1. It is my understanding that the BLM is working to implement the recommendations in the June 2013 OIG audit and the December 2013 GAO report, which raised concerns that leases in several states appear to have been leased at less than fair market value, resulting in less revenue for both federal and state coffers. The problems identified in that report must be addressed. The royalties paid by coal companies—and energy development of all kinds on federal lands—provide critical support for local schools, roads and other services that Colorado families count on.

However, there is an appropriate balance that ensures that the government is paid fairly while providing applicants with a decision in a timely manner. Some of my constituents have expressed concerns that while BLM is revamping its lease application approval process, delays in processing applications are creating economic hardship that may result in job losses and delay additional hiring.

Can you provide specific examples of the actions BLM has/is taking to address the audit and report recommendations and steps that BLM is taking to improve the permitting of mine leases?

QUESTIONS FOR NEIL KORNZE FROM SENATOR MURKOWSKI

Question 1. The President continues to tout oil and gas development from NPR-A as part of his "all of the above" energy strategy, but beyond holding lease sales, it is not clear to me what the Administration is doing to help ensure a project in the petroleum reserve may be successfully developed. I have followed the Greater Moose's Tooth 1 project very closely. If approved, this will be the first production from NPR-A. The project is expected to add 30,000 barrels of oil per day to TAPS. And given the annual 5-6-percent decline in throughput, GMT-1 is vital to TAPS continued operation. Can you describe how you see the National Petroleum Reserve-Alaska fitting into the President's energy strategy?

Question 2. Why have there been significant difficulties encountered by your agency regarding oil and gas Environmental Impact Statements not being able to withstand judicial review?

Question 3. I know your agency is working with the Fish and Wildlife and others in preparation for a decision on listing Sage Grouse next September. Such a listing could have significant impacts on energy production on public lands. What is the status of your agency's contribution to the decision making process? Given the enormous amount of analysis that must be undertaken to make such a decision, is there enough time to make an adequate determination?

QUESTION FOR NEIL KORNZE FROM SENATOR HELLER

Question 1. The National Association of Counties are strong supporters of the legislation, in large part to the additional resources the royalty laid out in the bill would generate for public lands counties.

There is a small concern that the agency would take these revenues into account when calculating PILT payments. The sponsors' intention is for these dollars to supplement PILT, not be used as a replacement.

How would the BLM interpret the current language?

Additional Material Submitted for the Record

STATEMENT OF THE AMERICAN WIND ENERGY ASSOCIATION, ON S. 279

On behalf of the over 1,000 members of the American Wind Energy Association (AWEA[1]), we appreciate the opportunity to share our views on S. 279, the "Public Lands Renewable Energy Development Act of 2013."

AWEA is generally supportive of the existing right-of-way and rental fee structure for siting on BLM lands. On paper, at least, it is a reasonable process that results in a fair return to taxpayers. The industry has much less experience with the Forest Service. Only a single wind project has ever been permitted on Forest Service land, and it has not yet been constructed.

That said, even under the current processes for BLM and the Forest Service, it is much more complex, takes longer, and costs more to develop wind energy projects on public lands than private lands. That is why 98.6% of the currently installed wind energy capacity is on private lands.

AWEA is concerned that moving to competitive leasing will add complexity, time and expense, and in turn uncertainty, to developing on public lands, which will continue the trend of wind energy developers looking elsewhere. It is particularly complex for wind energy, which requires 1-2 years of testing for wind speeds before a company can determine whether a site is economically viable to develop or not. It is unlikely wind energy companies will bid for the right to put up a meteorological tower to test wind speeds without any explicit right to later apply to construct at that site. At the same time, it will be difficult to bid on a site as a package—the right to put up the tower that also comes with a right to apply to construct—without having the wind speed data up front, which cannot be accurately obtained without on-site testing.

AWEA recognizes and appreciates the intent of the bill supporters in making wind energy permitting more closely mirror other activities permitted on public lands and to ensure a fair return to taxpayers. The bill does include some worthy elements that AWEA supports, including directing a portion of the revenue paid by wind and solar projects back into BLM and state agencies to improve permitting for additional projects, sharing revenue with states and counties, and providing funds for conservation. However, AWEA is unsure that the 15 percent allocation for improved permitting will provide sufficient resources for this purpose, particularly given needs of the U.S. Fish and Wildlife Service and state agencies, and would appreciate the opportunity to further discuss this with the committee. S. 279 also includes helpful language changes that address some concerns raised by AWEA on previous versions of the bill. However, AWEA recommends additional changes; these recommendations are outlined below.

Further, it is important to understand the impact of S. 279 will be marginal, at best, if Congress fails to renew the production tax credit (PTC) for renewable energy, and create a long-term stable tax policy which treats all energy producers equally. Keeping taxes low on wind energy has contributed to a major American success story.

Status of wind energy in the U.S.

The U.S. wind industry:

- Has attracted over $15 billion annually in investment into U.S. communities over the past 5 years;

---

[1] AAWEA is the national trade association representing a broad range of entities with a common interest in encouraging the deployment and expansion of wind energy resources in the United States. AWEA's members include wind turbine manufacturers, component suppliers, project developers, project owners and operators, financiers, researchers, renewable energy supporters, utilities, marketers, customers and their advocates.

- Supports more than 50,000 U.S. jobs; and,
- Has more than 550 manufacturing facilities in 44 states supplying the industry.

Wind energy is widely available. Presently, there are 61 gigawatts of wind energy installed in 39 states and Puerto Rico. Wind energy projects are being developed in many of the remaining 11 states without utility scale wind turbines, and several of those states are currently buying wind energy from outside their states to serve their customers because it is the lowest cost option available.

Wind energy is affordable. DOE data shows the average cost of wind energy has fallen 43 percent over the last four years, and that electric rates have increased less than half as much in the 10 states with the most wind energy compared to the 40 that have lesser amounts or none.

Wind energy is reliable. On an average annual basis, wind energy already provides more than 25% of the electricity in two states and 10% or more in nine states. At the regional level, wind energy at times has provided upwards of 20% to 40% of electric generation in the plains states, Texas, California and the Pacific Northwest. All of this is without reliability concerns.

Specific suggestions for S. 279

1. The transition language should be more specific that projects under development on public lands under the existing system will be grandfathered and not be subject to competitive leasing: Developers have pursued right-of-way authorizations in good faith, including spending significant time and dollars to collect data on wind speeds, conduct environmental reviews and other preliminary activities. It creates too much business uncertainty and investment risk, and, frankly, is not fair, to change the ground rules mid-process and make such sites available to the highest bidder.

Although page 17, lines 12-25, and page 18, lines 1-12, establishes that existing projects will be grandfathered under the existing rules, this section as currently written limits this to projects that have filed a Plan of Development (POD).

Besides existing Right-of-Ways (ROW) that have been granted, AWEA proposes grandfathering any project that has a pending: (1) application for a ROW at the time any wind energy competitive leasing pilot program is established and, if that project is subsequently granted a permit, files for a Plan of Development (POD) within one year of expiration of the ROW permit; or (2) an application for site testing or development ROW as of the date the final regulations for the wind energy competitive leasing program are issued and submits a POD within one year of expiration of the ROW permit.

Existing ROW grants must be honored and holders of a Type II ROW for site testing should retain the right of first refusal to apply for Type III ROW for construction and operation without being subject to competitive leasing provisions.

Type II ROWs should be renewable for an unlimited number of times so long as a Type III ROW is being processed and a Plan of Development (POD) has been submitted.

Holders of Type III ROWs should also be allowed to proceed under the current rules and should not be subject to competition on an existing ROW. The need to accommodate these circumstances can be seen, for example, in a case where a developer with a Type II ROW needs more time to make the decision regarding whether to proceed with a Type III ROW application.

Furthermore, Page 10, lines 23-25 and Page 11, lines 1-7, gives credit in a competitive lease sale under the proposed pilot program for projects with a pending application. As indicated above, projects with a pending application should not be part of the proposed pilot program and instead should be grandfathered under the existing system.

2. Clarify the definition of a notice of intent with regards to ineligible sites: The language on Page 8, lines 4-7, indicates that sites where a notice of intent has been issued will not be selected for the pilot program. AWEA recommends clarification regarding what this notice of intent is with respect to BLM or the Forest Service.

AWEA appreciates the opportunity to provide comments on this legislation. We look forward to working with the subcommittee on this important issue.

STATEMENT OF SHAWN BOLTON, RIO BLANCO COUNTY, COMMISSIONER, CCI BOARD OF DIRECTORS, PRESIDENT, AND JOHN MARTIN, GARFIELD COUNTY, COMMISSIONER, WESTERN INTERSTATE REGION, PRESIDENT, PUBLIC LANDS COMMITTEE, COLORADO COUNTIES INC., CHAIR

Dear Senate Udall,

On behalf of Colorado Counties, Inc. (CCI), I am writing to express our support of the Public Lands Renewable Energy Development Act (S. 279). This legislation extends royalties and lease income from solar and wind projects developed on Federal lands to home states and counties.

Similar to existing revenue sharing models for alternative energy development, for example, geothermal, the Act would share revenues with states and counties, while providing reinvestment in BLM renewable energy programs and sharing critical funds to sustain wildlife and recreational uses of nearby land. Revenues sharing arrangements with local governments are needed to support county operations impacted by local energy development and production.

Countless counties nationwide have Federal lands within their boundaries that have been developed or are suitable for alternative energy development. Counties have historically been indispensable advocates for the development of alternative energy production in the United States. Future revenue sharing dollars will contribute to the delivery of critical governmental services and the development of much needed capital improvement projects such as road maintenance, public safety and law enforcement, conservation easements, capital for leveraging federal and state resources, and the critical stabilization of operations budgets in tough economic times.

Again, CCI applauds the introduction of the Public Land Renewable Energy Development Act of 2013 and respectfully ask for swift passage of this landmark legislation.

———

STATEMENT OF COLORADO TROUT UNLIMITED * SAN JUAN ANGLER * SCOTT FLY RODS * GLOBAL WETLANDS * REP YOUR WATER * DVORAK EXPEDITIONS * THE SPORTSMAN OUTDOORS * THEODORE ROOSEVELT CONSERVATION PARTNERSHIP * COLORADO WILDLIFE FEDERATION * CONFLUENCE CASTING * MAYFLY MEDIA/FLY FISHING FILM TOUR * WESTERN ANGLING PROPERTIES * WATERFALL RANCH OUTFITTERS * FORT LEWIS COLLEGE FLY FISHING CLUB * DURANGLERS FLIES & SUPPLIES * BULL MOOSE SPORTSMEN * COLORADO BACKCOUNTRY HUNTERS AND ANGLERS

We write on behalf of thousands of Colorado hunters and anglers in support of the Public Lands Renewable Energy Development Act. We appreciate your support for this legislation, and ask that you continue working to advance the bills during the remainder of this year.

Colorado's public lands provide some of our best opportunities to hunt and fish. These same public lands also hold great potential for wind and solar energy development. In fact, Colorado is one of six western states with designated public land solar energy development zones. We support the development of renewable energy resources on public lands as long as it is done in the right places and in a manner that conserves fish and wildlife habitat.

The provisions of the Public Lands Renewable Energy Development Act that establish a pilot leasing program for wind and solar energy development on public lands and apply a substantial portion of royalty revenue to offsetting impacts to fish and wildlife habitat and hunting and fishing access are essential to balancing development and hunting and fishing opportunities. The Public Lands Renewable Energy Development Act would help wind and solar development move forward on appropriate public lands in a way that sustains our sporting heritage.

Support for this legislation is broad. In addition to sportsmen, the bill is supported by Colorado Counties, Inc., the Southwest Colorado Council of Governments, and the Western Governors' Association, among others. Again we thank you for supporting this important legislation, and we look forward to working with you to move the bill through the legislative process this year.

———

STATEMENT OF DAN NAATZ, VICE PRESIDENT, FEDERAL RESOURCES, THE INDEPENDENT PETROLEUM ASSOCIATION OF AMERICA

The Independent Petroleum Association of America (IPAA) supports S. 2440, the "BLM Permit Processing Improvement Act of 2014," and urges the Senate Committee on Energy and Natural Resources to take quick action on this important legislation.

IPAA is a national trade association representing the thousands of independent oil and natural gas explorers and producers, as well as the service and supply industries that support their efforts. Independent producers drill about 95 percent of American oil and natural gas wells; produce more than 50 percent of American oil, and more than 85 percent of American natural gas.

"The BLM Permit Processing Improvement Act" is a bipartisan piece of legislation that reauthorizes and makes reforms to the successful BLM pilot project initiative authorized in the Energy Policy Act of 2005 (EPACT). It is vital that the Senate take action on this legislation during the 113th Congress because the program has a 10-year sunset provision and is set to expire in 2015. U.S. shale oil and natural gas development has been a game changer for our nation's energy picture. Efficient production on federal lands will not only help enhance American energy security, but provide millions of dollars of much-needed revenue to federal and state governments.

The pilot office program has a proven track record of success in the seven field offices where it was originally implemented under EPACT. When the program was launched, the seven offices identified in EPACT processed nearly 70 percent of the applications for permits to drill (APD) that were received by the BLM. This legislation expands on that successful model and improves the program by providing additional flexibility to the Secretary of the Interior to designate new project offices, accounting for shifting industry priorities as new plays are discovered on federal lands. The bill also allows the APD fee to remain at the BLM state office, providing the agency even more flexibility to respond to activity levels and responsibilities.

Production of oil and natural gas on federal lands will remain a key part of America's energy portfolio in the coming years. In addition, this exploration and production benefits the U.S. economy through job growth, government revenues, and enhanced American energy security. However, oil and natural gas production on federal lands continues to decline, and BLM permitting times get ever-longer. Last month, the Department of the Interior released a report from its own Inspector General's (IG) office citing inefficiencies with the BLM permitting process. Specifically, the IG report found that inefficiencies within the BLM impede production, dates for completion of individual APDs are rarely set or enforced, and the review process may continue indefinitely. The report found that on average the APD approval process on BLM lands takes 228 calendar days, and in many offices around the Intermountain West, the numbers are much higher. Although S. 2440 will not be able to solve all of the issues outlined in the IG's report, it can make a significant difference in addressing key permitting questions.

IPAA would like to thank Senators Tom Udall and John Barrasso for their leadership regarding S. 2440. We would also like to thank the Chair of the Energy and Natural Resources Committee Mary Landrieu, Ranking Member Lisa Murkowski and all of the members of the Committee for making passage of this important bill a priority.

Industry's goal is, and has always been to achieve reasonable time frames for APD processing on public lands and reduce undue permitting backlogs. This bipartisan legislation is a commonsense measure that will help achieve that goal. The bill is the result of long, bipartisan negotiations in which all parties had to compromise to achieve results. The bill reflects the best traditions of the Senate, and we ask that the Energy Committee move this legislation to the Senate floor as soon as possible.

––––––––

STATEMENT OF BOBBY MCENANEY, SENIOR DEPUTY DIRECTOR OF WESTERN RENEWABLES PROJECT, NATURAL RESOURCES DEFENSE COUNCIL

Dear Chairman Landrieu and Ranking Member Murkowski,

The Natural Resources Defense Council (NRDC) appreciates this opportunity to submit comments to the Senate Committee on Energy and Natural Resources in its work to consider additional opportunities to improve how federal renewable resources are permitted on the public lands managed by the Bureau of Land Management (BLM). NRDC and its over one million members and activists support the responsible siting of renewable resources on the nation's public lands, particularly as a means to address the tangible and negative consequences poised by global climate change, whether such development is from wind, solar, or geothermal energy. NRDC also strongly supports the protection and conservation of our nation's incomparable natural landscapes that bestow our nation with immeasurable benefits.

Given these multiple goals, NRDC has worked diligently to support mechanisms that strive to deploy renewables in a manner that also protects the nation's most sensitive lands and wildlife. By embracing a "Smart from the Start" approach, which diligently contemplates and anticipates the best places to site renewables in a more deliberate fashion while also protecting ecological important areas, it has been demonstrated that such a process can be key to achieving the dual goal of encouraging renewable energy development and conservation. But additional tools and mechanisms will be necessary in order to permanently ensure that the recent and substantial gains that have been achieved in deploying renewables on BLM lands can continue in a meaningful manner.

For these reasons, NRDC supports S. 279, the Public Land and Renewable Energy Development Act of 2013 (PLREDA). This important legislation is a critical step in modernizing the methods the BLM employs in permitting and managing solar and wind energy resources. The legislation seeks to improve the current BLM permitting system for wind and solar by proposing a series remedies that would phase out a number archaic and institutionalized regulatory mechanisms that are currently inadequate in addressing the needs of renewable energy development while also adequately balancing the additional environmental, economic, and social considerations incurred from wind and solar generation.

Fundamentally, the BLM system for permitting renewable resources is encumbered by an antiquated administrative construct. This is due to the fact that Congress has prescribed that onshore federal wind and solar resources are to be managed under Title V of the Federal Land Policy and Management Act,[1] which advises that permits to lease these resources are to be treated as linear-right-of-ways (ROWs). A linear right-of-way lease under Title V is a temporary conveyance whose administrative underpinnings date back to the 19th century, where ROWs were permitted primarily for linear applications and other like infrastructure including roads, ditches, and railways. Agency discretion to modify these permits was an inherent part of the ROW construct, granting the agency needed flexibility to move and/or modify ROW permits when circumstances dictated. Given that a ROW does not convey a right, but merely a privilege, the BLM retains a great deal of administerial latitude in reserving the right to modify, suspend, relocate or even terminate (under certain prescribed conditions) a ROW permit. However, the regulations of ROWs did not anticipate the technological needs and scale associated with the generation of utility scale solar and wind resources, nor the permanency associated with such investments. Hence, solar and wind developers are severely disadvantaged by the fact that the BLM retains broad latitude to potentially modify investments made by renewable energy developers. Given the substantial and permanent nature of utility scale renewable infrastructure, such a level of regulatory uncertainty undermines the efforts to scale renewables on federal lands.

In contrast, the management of fluid minerals—derived from longstanding mineral law—has established that leases confer a compensable right or interest once issued, which cannot be summarily terminated (without due cause on part of the managing agency). And even then, a lease holder is often entitled to compensation if a lease is cancelled by an agency. From a purely financial perspective, a mineral lease holds greater attraction than a ROW given the financial and temporal certainty that is provided by possessing such an interest.

The other practical difference between a mineral lease and a ROW is related to the differing financial obligations that must be met, as demonstrated by the following table:

---

[1] 43 U.S.C. §§1701-1785

FINANCIAL OBILGATIONS: MINERAL LEASES versus ONSHORE
RENEWABLE ROWs[2]

	Mineral Lease	Onshore Renewable ROW
Competitive Lease	Yes, in most cases—price is determined by fair market value	No—first come, first serve basis
Cost Recovery for Project Applications[3]	Varies depending on feedstock	Minimal. As low as $100 to file a ROW application
Rental	Yes—minimal, as low as $1.50 an acre annually	Yes—Annual rents for solar range from $17 an acre to as high as $6,897 an acre. Wind rentals are approximately half as low as solar.
Royalty	Yes—varies depending on feedstock, but for most energy types, it is fixed at no less than 12.5%	No

[2] This chart is derived from: Pamela Baldwin, "Fair Market Value for Wind and Solar Development on Public Land," November 2010. Accessed July 26, 2014, at http://wilderness.org/sites/default/files/Fair-Market-Value-Whitepaper.pdf
[3] Does not include NEPA permitting costs

Of all these items, the most notable difference is the fact that mineral leases are required to pay a royalty. In contrast, the largest financial obligation of a ROW permit is associated with a rental. Royalties, from NRDC's perspective, are a superior way to track and assess projects given that they are technologically neutral and only assess power that is generated. In addition, given the methodology that the BLM has used to determine rentals for varying solar technologies, the current BLM rental scheme penalizes more efficient solar technologies that use less land than other comparable solar collection methods, such as concentrated solar projects.[4]

Given these aforementioned inadequacies, S. 279 grants the BLM the discretion to contemplate the adoption of additional mechanisms that could result in the transition to a competitive, royalty-based leasing system that treats wind and solar generation much the same as oil, geothermal, and gas. With the adoption of such a royalty system, PLREDA would establish a number of mechanisms that would direct revenues generated to further facilitate the responsible development of wind and solar resources. First, a portion royalty revenues would be directed to the states and counties where a project is developed, providing an additional incentive for these communities to partner with developers and land managers in promoting the development of renewables in their communities. In addition, the legislation also provides greater certainty for developers by dedicating a portion of receipts collected from rents and royalties to support better decision making by the agencies by funding planning, monitoring, and data collection. The same funds would also be directed toward the efficient processing of permit applications, which is quite similar to the Permit Process Improvement Fund that oil and gas development benefits from currently.

Lastly, and most critically from a conservation perspective, S. 279 also proposes a mechanism that would establish a mitigation system by dedicating a small portion of receipts to measures that would enhance the conservation of natural resources as a means to offset the inevitable impacts associated with large scale renewable energy development. We believe that a royalty system, in concert with locality and mitigation payments, is a superior process to ensure that the communities and habitats that will be host to renewable energy development are compensated in a fashion that will address and mitigate for some of the inevitable impacts associated with energy development—for development that will take place at an unprecedented scale. This also provides opportunities for developers to achieve the goals of becoming good stewards and good neighbors. The current rental system unfortunately does not provide these kinds of payments, and none of the receipts from the BLM rental

[4] See: "Uncle Sam, Solar Landlord, Is Under Fire," New York Times, http://green.blogs.nytimes.com/2010/06/17/uncle-sam-solar-landlord-is-under-fire/

system are provided for mitigation, locality payments, or adequate cost recovery. And nearly as important, by shifting to a leasing system, land managers can work with communities and developers to diligently identify in a prescribed manner what areas should be offered for leasing based upon the richness of the renewable resource, while also weighing the relative environmentally suitability to host such large scale development.

For these reasons, we again want to express our support for the Public Land and Renewable Energy Development Act of 2013 and appreciate this opportunity to submit comments for the record. Sincerely, Bobby McEnaney Senior Deputy Director of Western Renewables Project Natural Resources Defense Council

―――――

STATEMENT OF MICHAEL YOHN, CHAIRMAN, SAN LUIS VALLEY COUNTY COMMISSIONERS ASSOCIATION, ALAMOSA, CONEJOS, COSTILLA, MINERAL, RIO GRANDE, SAGUACHE COUNTIES

Dear Representative Tipton, Senator Udall, Senator Bennet:
The San Luis Valley County Commissioners Association would like to thank you for your support of the Public Lands Renewable Energy Development Act (HR 596 and S279). This legislation will level the playing field by requiring renewable energy resource development to pay a fair share of the revenues created through energy production just like other forms of energy development.

This legislation is fair and balanced and it will provide states and counties with revenues to help mitigate the impacts renewable energy development will have on their communities. Additionally, it will provide revenues by which the Department of the Interior can use to help pay for the cost of administering those industries.

The proposed legislation will also support the common goals of water resource protection and fish and wildlife conservation, through habitat restoration and protection and through improved public access. All of which are priority concerns for the residents of Colorado.

Our only concern regarding this Act is that it not modify PILT, or affect any PILT payment amounts, or the Secure Rural Schools Act payments in any way. Payments to the counties from royalties, generated from renewable energy resources must be in addition to PILT. We would also like to take this opportunity to let you know that we oppose any reductions in PILT payments due to gains from any other Federal Revenue Sharing programs.

Because of the importance of this Bill, we encourage you to take appropriate actions that will move this legislation through the legislative process. Again, we thank you for cosponsoring this important legislation and we look forward to working with you as the legislation moves forward.

―――――

STATEMENT OF MICHAEL E. WHITING, CHAIRMAN, SOUTHWEST COLORADO COUNCIL OF GOVERNMENTS

Dear Senator Udall,
The Southwest Colorado Council of Governments (SWCCOG) would like express our support for the Public Lands Renewable Energy Development Act (S. 279). The five counties of Archuleta, Dolores, La Plata, Montezuma, and San Juan contain over 1.6 million acres of public lands, including Mesa Verde National Park. Much of these lands are suitable for alternative energy development.

As you know, this legislation will require renewable energy resource development to pay royalties from energy production on renewable energy projects on Federal lands. Providing reinvestment in renewable energy programs while sharing funds for the support of waterways, wildlife habitat, and recreational uses is a benefit for all citizens.

The potential future revenue will help the five counties of the SWCCOG provide critical governmental services, help fund the backlog of infrastructure improvement projects, and stabilize budgets still impacted by slow growth and the economic recession. Furthermore, these revenues will also help counties manage the impacts of energy development.

The 12 municipalities and 5 counties of Southwest Colorado Council of Governments are committed to working with the Federal government as partners to encourage sound, responsible energy development. The expansion of alternate energy industries through this legislation will help create a more sustainable regional economy while protecting our public lands and our way of life.

Thank you for your strong support of the Public Lands Renewable Energy Development Act.

STATEMENT OF CHASE HUNTLEY, SENIOR DIRECTOR OF GOVERNMENT RELATIONS FOR ENERGY, THE WILDERNESS SOCIETY

Dear Chairwoman Landrieu and Ranking Member Murkowski,

The Wilderness Society appreciates the opportunity to submit this statement in regard to energy permitting and development on public lands managed by the Bureau of Land Management. The Wilderness Society works on behalf of its 500,000 members and supporters to protect wilderness and inspire Americans to care for our wild places. This includes working to ensure that the development of needed new energy resources is done in a way that protects wild lands, recreational opportunities, and local communities.

We support efforts to sustainably develop energy resources found on our public lands and forests. As with any form of development, not all places are appropriate for energy projects. Some places are simply too wild or too sensitive to develop. And where development occurs, it must take place in a responsible manner and impacts fully offset to ensure the health and safety of local community and other land users.

We do not believe that there is a logjam for energy development permits for our public lands -our experience is that permitting is moving apace, and efforts underway at the agency promise to further enhance the efficiency and effectiveness of permitting efforts. Following are our views on the bills that are the focus of today's discussion. Thank you for the opportunity to offer this statement for the record.

ATTACHMENT

Public Lands Renewable Energy Development Act

The Public Lands Renewable Energy Development Act (S. 279) presents a conservative, balanced approach to ensuring renewable energy resources are developed in a manner that safeguards and enhances the health of our public lands, counties and recreational opportunities. The bill provides land managers with additional direction and authorities to aid in developing clean energy projects on public lands.

Under the bill, federal land managers would consider how best to develop these resources to the benefit of taxpayers, project proponents and other land users. In particular, the bill proposes a move to a lease-based system, rather than rights-of-way currently in use. Such a system has been advocated by industry watchers,[1] the solar industry,[2] and public land law scholars[3] as providing greater certainty for all parties. And the bill considers whether alternative fee structures, such as a royalty, would be more appropriate for these industries in lieu of the current rental system, which has been criticized by the industry and other stakeholders. The bill has the potential to modernize wind and solar development on public lands. It can help put renewable energy on a level playing field with energy sources that have been developed on public lands for over a century, which have thrived on public lands in part due to the stable leasing system in place.

Importantly, the bill would establish a mechanism to reinvest in the counties, states and communities most impacted by projects. It reauthorizes the current system of payments for geothermal energy development, and creates a similar system for counties and states from the rents or royalties collected from wind and solar development. These funds are needed to address the concerns that infrastructure, public services and quality of life are stressed by the intense activities that come with utility-scale renewable energy development.

The bill also creates a system that returns a portion of rents and royalties from wind and solar to improving permitting that can help make it more efficient to review and process applications. These funds would support the data collection, monitoring and planning activities essential to smart permitting decisions, and would be available for transfer to cooperating agencies as well. This provision is similar to the Permit Process Improvement Fund already available for oil and gas development.

---

[1] E.g., see Scott Bank, "Practical Advice: Wind and Solar Projects on BLM (Bureau of Land Management) Lands," Project Finance Newsletter. Chadbourne & Parke LLP. November 2011. Accessed July 26, 2014, at http://www.chadbourne.com/practicaladvice_bureau_of_land_management_nov11_projectfinance/.

[2] Solar Energy Industries Association, "Comments to BLM on Proposed Rulemaking Regarding Competitive Process for Leasing Public Lands for Solar and Wind Development." February 2012. Accessed July 26, 2014, at http://www.seia.org/research-resources/comments-blm-proposed-rule-making-regarding-competitive-process-leasing-public.

[3] Pamela Baldwin, "Fair Market Value for Wind and Solar Development on Public Land," November 2010. Accessed July 26, 2014, at http://wilderness.org/sites/default/files/Fair-Market-Value-Whitepaper.pdf

Most significantly, the bill makes a commitment to enhance natural resource conservation and stewardship as a part of renewable energy development and production. The bill establishes a fish and wildlife conservation fund that would support expanding recreational access, conservation and restoration work and other important stewardship activities. In the face of shrinking federal resources, these funds are essential to keep pace with the new challenges facing federal and state land managers. These conservation investments would not supplant or compete with traditional mitigation, but would instead create the opportunity to improve our lands and waters as we develop energy resources. Putting revenue already collected from renewable energy to work for conservation will link conservationists, sportsmen, recreationists and the renewable energy industry together.

BLM Permit Processing Improvement Act

The BLM Permit Processing Improvement Act (S. 2440) reauthorizes and modifies the BLM Permit Processing Improvement Fund created by the Energy Policy Act of 2005. We applaud the bill author and original cosponsors for their efforts to enhance the efficiency and improve the environmental outcomes for oil and gas drilling on public lands. We are supportive of efforts to keep dedicated agency staff with necessary skills and experience in these offices. Importantly, these offices address a broad range of issues well beyond processing applications for permits to drill—but also monitor reclamation efforts and spill cleanup, oversee diligence, and conduct inspections and enforcement activities. We believe the bill could be substantially strengthened by expanding the range of activities covered by the Improvement Fund-specifically the Rental Account-to include all the necessary activities undertaken by these offices. In particular, this should include inspections and enforcement activities which recent independent investigators have found is sorely in need of attention but for which the agency has stated it simply does not have sufficient resources.

STATEMENT OF TEX G. HALL, CHAIRMAN MANDAN, HIDATSA AND ARIKARA NATION OF THE FORT BERTHOLD RESERVATION, NEW TOWN, ND

Chairwoman Landrieu, Ranking Member Murkowski, and Members of the Committee on Energy and Natural Resources, thank you for the opportunity to testify on "Breaking the Logjam at BLM: Examining Ways to More Efficiently Process Permits for Energy Production on Federal Lands." My name is Tex Hall. I am the Chairman of the Mandan Hidatsa and Arikara Nation (MHA Nation) of the Fort Berthold Reservation.

Although this hearing is focused on the Bureau of Land Management (BLM) and energy permitting on Federal lands, one of the bills before the Committee, S. 2440, the BLM Permit Processing Improvement Act of 2014, would have a dramatic impact on energy development on Indian lands. As currently drafted, S. 2440 would increase Application for Permit to Drill (APD) fees on Indian lands, but would not provide any benefits for energy permitting on Indian lands.

As I explain in my testimony, the MHA Nation requests that the Committee amend S. 2440 to include a proposal developed by the Coalition of Large Tribes (COLT) to create an Indian Energy Regulatory Office that would provide the leadership and agency coordination we need for Indian energy permitting. This new Office would utilize existing resources and could be supported by S. 2440's proposed increase APD fees. If amended to include the entire COLT proposal, S. 2440 would provide long needed improvements to energy permitting on Indian lands.

The MHA Nation has a detailed understanding of the Federal energy permitting process and the need for improvements. The MHA Nation's Fort Berthold Reservation sits in the heart of the Bakken Formation-the most active oil and gas play in the United States. Currently, on our Reservation there are 30 drilling rigs, more than 27,000 semi-trucks, and about 1,300 oil and gas wells producing in excess of 300,000 barrels of oil per day. Our Reservation, located in west-central North Dakota, is the equivalent of the 7th highest producing oil and gas state in the Country.

The MHA Nation has struggled with BLM, the Bureau of Indian Affairs (BIA) and other Federal agencies for every single energy permit needed to get these wells into production. For too long, Indian energy permitting has been subject to a bureaucratic maze of Federal agencies. Former Senator Dorgan estimated that each individual oil and gas permit had to make its way through 4 agencies and a 49-step process. We now count 7 agencies and 100 or more steps.

As currently drafted, S. 2440 would further increase the barriers to Indian energy development by raising APD fees to $9,500. The BLM applies APD fees to energy permits on Indian lands even though our lands are not Federal public lands. Instead of increasing barriers to Indian energy development, the MHA Nation asks that S. 2440 be amended to include the entire COLT proposal for an Indian Energy Regulatory Office and use funding from the increased fees to benefit energy permit processing on Indian lands.

The COLT proposal mirrors the successes of BLM's Federal Permit Coordination Offices created by Section 365 of the Energy Policy Act of 2005 but provides an office focused on development of Indian energy resources. This Office would utilize existing Department of the Interior resources located in Denver, Colorado to streamline and coordinate energy permitting on Indian lands. The COLT proposal is attached my testimony along with resolutions from COLT and NCAI approving the proposal.

There are a variety of reasons the Committee should amend S. 2440 to include the entire COLT proposal and take this opportunity to improve energy permitting on Indian lands. First, it is time to bring the federal government's oversight and management of Indian energy resources into the 21st Century. The Indian Energy Regulatory Office proposed by COLT would provide the leadership, staff and expertise needed for coordinated review of Indian energy permits across the Federal government.

Second, as currently drafted, S. 2440 increases APD fees on Indian lands to $9,500, but none of this funding is used to support energy permitting on Indian lands. Instead, all of the funding would go to BLM's Federal Permit Coordination Offices and permitting on Federal lands. APD fees are already a burden for energy development on Indian lands. Under S. 2440, energy development on Indian land gets all of the burdens and none of the benefits. We ask that the entire COLT proposal be included in the bill and that APD fees be used to support an Indian Energy Regulatory Office.

Third, Congress, at a minimum, should give energy development on Indian lands the same attention and focus as energy development on Federal lands. The benefits of energy development on Indian lands far exceed the benefits of energy development on Federal lands, yet Congress has done little to improve energy permitting on Indian lands. Energy development on Indian lands provides needed jobs and training, economic development, and, if managed properly, long-term investment in reservation infrastructure. With increased revenues and resources, tribal governments are also able to provide vital services to our members.

Finally, the COLT proposal should be included as separate section in S. 2440 to specifically address energy permitting on Indian lands. Indian lands and BIA responsibilities cannot simply be included as a part of the existing BLM Offices. Indian lands are not public lands, yet the Tribe must fight every day to prevent Federal agencies from applying public land management standards to Indian lands. We need legislation to create a new office that is focused on Indian lands.

The Indian Energy Regulatory Office proposed by COLT would be guided by basic principles of Federal Indian law that have been lost in the current unorganized system for overseeing energy development on Federal Indian trust lands. The Office would treat Indian lands according to federal trust management standards and would provide technical support to tribes as we enter a new era of self-determination and we manage and regulate energy development ourselves.

The MHA Nation asks that you act quickly to amend S. 2440 to include the entire COLT proposal for an Indian Energy Regulatory Office. Amending the bill to include the COLT proposal would not only avoid damaging energy development on our Reservation, and a number of other Indian reservations, but would also provide needed improvements to energy permitting on Indian lands. The MHA Nation looks forward to working with the Committee to make needed changes to S. 2440. Thank you for the opportunity to provide this testimony.

––––––––

STATEMENT OF CHRIS WOOD, TROUT UNLIMITED, ARLINGTON, VA

Chairwoman Landrieu and Ranking Member Murkowski,

I write on behalf of Trout Unlimited (TU) and its 155,000 members to thank you for holding a hearing on S. 279, the Public Lands Renewable Energy Development Act. I ask that this letter be included in the hearing record.

TU strongly supports the Public Lands Renewable Energy Development Act because it can help set us on a path to responsible energy development that takes care of the interests of hunters and anglers, and the fish and wildlife habitat we depend on.

Wind and solar energy projects are a relatively new, but growing presence on western public lands. Since the beginning of 2009, 29 solar projects totaling more than 8,000 megawatts, and 11 wind projects totaling more than 4,000 megawatts, have been approved on public lands in the U.S.

TU supports responsible energy development on public lands. We take pride in our efforts to work with traditional energy developers and federal land managers to ensure that development is balanced with fishing and hunting opportunities.

It is important to understand the context for energy development on public lands. Numerous stressors on the western landscape affect fish and wildlife habitat and hunting and angling opportunity. These include: traditional energy development, insect and disease outbreaks, intense and more frequent wildfire, invasive plants, private land development, and drought conditions in already over-subscribed basins. If we are going to add large-scale wind and solar development to this picture it must be done in a thoughtful way.

Processes such as the Solar Programmatic EIS, which identified zones suitable for development, are helping to guide sound siting decisions that avoid and minimize impacts to fish and wildlife habitat. Even with the best siting decisions, however, large-scale wind and solar projects will take up big chunks of land for long periods of time, and some impacts will be unavoidable. The Public Lands Renewable Energy Development Act provides an answer to this challenge.

The bill offers a way to offset unavoidable impacts on fish, wildlife, and water resources by creating a conservation fund derived from royalties and other revenues from public land wind and solar energy development. This conservation fund is essential to our ability to balance wind and solar energy development with the kind of unparalleled hunting and fishing opportunities that make our western public lands a prime destination for sportsmen and women from around the country.

The conservation fund would be used in regions where renewable energy development takes place so that work can be done to improve our lands and waters. For example, invasive plant treatment could be done to enhance big game habitat to improve the health of the herd. Projects to increase irrigation efficiency could be used to stretch the water supply and provide flows for fish, even as new water demands for energy development are met. Where an area previously used by hunters becomes a wind or solar project, voluntary access easements could be used to gain better access to surrounding public lands. If we have the resources to do these types of activities we will be able to balance wind and solar development with fishing and hunting opportunities on a landscape scale.

Finding a balance between wind and solar development and the conservation of fish and wildlife on public lands will be essential to the future of renewable energy on public lands. Wind and solar offer the prospect of much-needed jobs and increased energy security for our nation. We need for these benefits to coexist with the outstanding cultural and economic benefits of hunting and fishing. A survey by the Fish & Wildlife Service found that 91.1 million U.S. residents fished, hunted, or wildlife watched in 2011, and they spent $145 billion on their activities. This is a large, and growing, contributor to our economy: 11 percent more people fished in 2011 than in 2006, and 9 percent more people hunted. We need high quality, accessible habitat to sustain this economic activity. The conservation fund created by the Public Lands Renewable Energy Development Act would support the work needed to maintain our public land natural resource values.

The sportsmen's community is one that is naturally inclined to work collaboratively to solve problems. Trout Unlimited's 155,000 members annually dedicate more than 600,000 volunteer hours to conservation. Hunters and anglers are strong conservationists, and our members take great pride and joy in planting trees along streams, removing invasive plants, or working with agencies to reconnect streams. The Public Lands Renewable Energy Development Act, by providing the resources needed to do habitat improvement work in the field, will help position the sportsmen's community as partners as wind and solar projects are built on public lands.

I'm an angler, as are almost all Trout Unlimited members. Conservation is the most affirmative, hopeful, and optimistic idea that America ever gave the rest of the world. And fishing is inherently an act of optimism. Each time you cast a fly, it is with the hope that you are about to hook a fish-even if your last 100 casts have come up empty. That spirit of optimism permeates Trout Unlimited's work. We clean up abandoned mines and get fish back into streams where they had been wiped out for decades. We work with ranchers to conserve water and restore trout to streams that had previously run dry. We partner with landowners to improve old water diversion structures and enable fish to reach upstream habitat. These projects start with the idea that we can make things better than they are today, and they succeed through hard work and cooperation.

The Public Lands Renewable Energy Development Act embodies this spirit of optimism. It is a demonstration of how people of good will can come together to apply common sense to common problems for the common good. With it we can develop energy resources, bolster local economies, diversify county revenue streams, and make the fishing and hunting better than we found it. That is why it has attracted the support of 60 cosponsors in the House, from both sides of the aisle and every point on the political spectrum. It is cosponsored by members of your committee from both parties.

Again I thank you for holding a hearing on S. 279. We appreciate the leadership of Senators Tester and Heller on this bill. And we look forward to working with you to advance the Public Lands Renewable Energy Development Act.

STATEMENT OF CHAIRMAN GORDON HOWELL, UTE TRIBAL BUSINESS COMMITTEE, UTE INDIAN TRIBE OF THE UINTAH AND OURAY RESERVATION

Chairwoman Landrieu, Ranking Member Murkowski, and Members of the Committee on Energy and Natural Resources, thank you for the opportunity to testify. My name is Gordon Howell. I am the Chairman of the Business Committee for the Ute Indian Tribe of the Uintah and Ouray Reservation. The Ute Indian Tribe consists of three Ute Bands: the Uintah, the Whiteriver and the Uncompahgre Bands. Our Reservation is located in northeastern Utah.

While this hearing was focused on the Bureau of Land Management (BLM) and energy permitting on Federal lands, one of the bills before the Committee, S. 2440, the BLM Permit Processing Improvement Act of 2014, would have a significant impact on energy development on Indian lands. As currently drafted, S. 2440 would increase Application for Permit to Drill (APD) fees for oil and gas development on Indian lands to $9,500 without providing any benefits to Indian energy development.

As you may know, the Bureau of Land Management (BLM) currently charges APD fees for permits to drill on Indian lands as well as Federal lands. On Indian lands this additional charge is yet another barrier to Indian energy development. Even worse, none of the funding BLM currently collects in APD fees benefits energy permitting on Indian lands. In fact, BLM's delays and inaction in processing permits on Indian lands is one of the biggest impediments to Indian energy development. S. 2440 would further this problem by increasing APD fees while still not providing support for energy permitting on Indian lands.

To resolve this issue, we ask that the Committee include in S. 2440 a proposal developed by the Coalition of Large Tribes' (COLT) and also adopted by the National Congress of American Indians (NCAI). The COLT proposal would create an Indian Energy Regulatory Office to mirror the success of BLM's Federal Permit Coordination Offices created by Section 365 of the Energy Policy Act of 2005 but provide an office focused on development of Indian energy resources. This Office would utilize existing Department of the Interior resources located in Denver, Colorado to streamline and coordinate energy permitting on Indian lands. The COLT proposal is attached my testimony along with resolutions from COLT and NCAI approving the proposal.

The Ute Indian Tribe, as well as many members of COLT, has a detailed understanding of the problems with energy permit processing and the solutions needed. The Ute Tribe is a major oil and gas producer. Production of oil and gas began on our Reservation in the 1940's and has been ongoing for the past 70 years with significant periods of expansion. The Tribe leases about 400,000 acres for oil and gas development. We have about 7,000 wells that produce 45,000 barrels of oil a day. We also produce about 900 million cubic feet of gas per day. And, we have plans for expansion. The Tribe is in process of opening up an additional 150,000 acres to mineral leases on our Reservation with an $80 million investment dedicated to exploration.

The Tribe relies on its oil and gas development as the primary source of funding for our tribal government and takes an active role in the development of its resources. However, despite our progress, the Tribe's ability to fully benefit from its resources is limited by the federal agencies overseeing oil and gas development on our Reservation. As the oil and gas companies who operate on our Reservation often tell the Tribe, the federal oil and gas permitting process is the single biggest risk factor to operations on the Reservation.

In order for the Tribe to continue to grow and expand our economy the federal permitting process needs to be streamlined and improved. For example, we need 10 times as many permits to be approved by the BLM and the Bureau of Indian Affairs. Currently, about 48 Applications for Permits to Drill (APD) are approved each year for oil and gas operations on our Reservation. We estimate that 450 APDs will be needed each year as we expand operations.

S. 2440 should be amended to avoid damaging the energy development we have worked so hard to create while also providing an opportunity to improve energy permitting on Indian lands. We ask that S. 2440 be amended to include the COLT proposal and specifically address Indian lands. As we describe below, there are a variety of reasons the Committee should take this opportunity to improve energy permitting on Indian lands.

First, it is time to bring the federal government's oversight and management of Indian energy resources into the 21st Century. For too long, Indian energy permitting has been subject to a bureaucratic maze of Federal agencies. Six years ago, former Senator Dorgan estimated that each individual oil and gas permit had to make its way through 4 agencies and a 49-step process. The Indian Energy Regulatory Office proposed by COLT would provide the leadership, staff and expertise needed for coordinated review of Indian energy permits across the Federal government.

Second, S. 2440 would increase APD fees to $9,500, but none of this funding would be used to support energy permitting on Indian lands. Instead, all of the funding would go to BLM's Federal Permit Coordination Offices and permitting on Federal lands. APD fees are already a burden for energy development on Indian lands. Under S. 2440, energy development on Indian land gets all of the burdens and none of the benefits. We ask that the COLT proposal be included in the bill and that APD fees be used to support an Indian Energy Regulatory Office.

Third, Congress, at a minimum, should give energy development on Indian lands the same attention and focus as energy development on Federal lands. The benefits of increased energy development on Indian lands far exceed the benefits of energy development on Federal lands, yet Congress has done little to improve energy permitting on Indian lands. Energy development on Indian lands provides needed jobs and training, economic development, and, if managed properly, long-term investment in reservation infrastructure. With increased revenues and resources, tribal governments are also able to provide vital services to our members.

Finally, the COLT proposal should be included as separate section in S. 2440 to specifically address energy permitting on Indian lands. Indian lands and the Bureau of Indian Affairs cannot simply be included as a part of the existing BLM Offices. Indian lands are not public lands, yet the Tribe must fight every day to prevent Federal agencies from applying public land management standards to Indian lands. We need legislation to create a new office that is focused on Indian lands.

The Indian Energy Regulatory Office proposed by COLT would be guided by basic principles of Federal Indian law that have been lost in the current unorganized system for overseeing energy development on Federal Indian trust lands. The Office would treat Indian lands according to federal trust management standards and would provide technical support to tribes as we enter a new era of self-determination and we manage and regulate energy development ourselves.

The Tribe asks that you act quickly to avoid damaging the energy development on our Reservation that we have worked so hard to create. The Tribe stands ready to work with the Committee on S. 2440 and to improve energy permitting on Indian lands. I would like to thank the Committee for the opportunity to present this testimony on behalf of the Ute Indian Tribe.

○